CROSS WORDS

CROSS WORDS
Sermons and Dramas for Lent

By

W. A. POOVEY

AUGSBURG PUBLISHING HOUSE
MINNEAPOLIS MINNESOTA

CROSS WORDS

Library of Congress Catalog Card No. 68-13421

Copyright acknowledgments are given in the Notes at the end of the book.

Scripture quotations are from the Revised Standard Version of the Bible, copyright 1946 and 1952 by the Division of Christian Education of the National Council of Churches.

Hymns from the *Service Book and Hymnal* (SBH) are used by permission of the Commission on the Liturgy and the Hymnal.

Manufactured in the United States of America

Introduction

The seven words of Christ from the cross have always fascinated the church. Even though the words are scattered through the four gospels, they have a certain unity and a definite sense of development. They start with a broad message of forgiveness and end with a final word when Jesus seems all alone with his heavenly Father. Because of their terseness of expression and depth of meaning, these seven statements have always been a fertile source of ideas for Lenten meditations and Good Friday services.

This book is the result of an experiment which blended drama and preaching in the context of congregational worship. Seven plays with contemporary settings, each followed by a sermon based on a word from the cross, were presented at Holy Trinity Lutheran Church in Dubuque, Iowa, and at Trinity Lutheran Church in Mason City, Iowa, during the Lenten season. The combination of play and sermon was intended to make real to the contemporary world the truth of the biblical words.

The plays were deliberately made easy to stage and to grasp, so that members of the congregations could participate in the worship service through drama. The sermons printed here were preached at Holy Trinity Lutheran Church, but any preacher could present his own message based on the biblical text and the play. In the sermons, allusions to the plays are minimal, so that the sermons may be read without a detailed knowledge of the plays. It is hoped that both plays and sermons will aid the Lenten worship of the church.

Contents

"Father, forgive them; for they know not what they do."

Luke 23:34

The First Word

The Forgiveness That Doesn't Stop

The Drama

THE CHARACTERS

MRS. STONELAND—a housewife, rather stout
MR. HARRIS—tall, a bitter scowl on his face
MRS. CAREY—thin, sharp-tongued
MRS. WOODY—stylish, rich

THE SETTING

Church interior. If short pews are available, use two or three. Otherwise, chairs arranged in several rows, on an angle in chancel. Characters are seated at opening. They may take their places during the singing of a hymn. Other people besides the four main characters may be included if desired. Each character rises and faces the congregation when his or her speech comes.

ALL: The group unites in the Lord's Prayer, concluding with the petition "Forgive us our trespasses as we forgive those who trespass against us."

MRS. STONELAND *(rising)*: My neighbor and I had a quarrel, and I don't ever intend to speak to her again. It was all about her flower beds. She does have pretty flowers—no wonder, she spends all of her time working with them—I could have pretty flowers too, only I have more important things to do. Three boys take a lot of work. It was the boys who started things, though she needn't to have been so cross. But she's an old maid. What can you expect?

I guess the boys did run through her yard lots of times. And they shouldn't have been playing where they could hit a ball into her flowers. But boys will be boys, and besides, she *had* heard me warn them not to play there. It wasn't *my* fault.

It *was* a shame that her biggest dahlia got trampled. I felt sorry about that. Still, she didn't have to yell at the boys and threaten to call the police. And I don't think she should have insisted that Fred give the boys a whipping when he came home. I told her so, too. Cranky old maid, I said. I know she didn't like that. I suppose that's why she demanded that I return the plate I borrowed from her when we had company. I would have sent it back sooner but I wanted to bake a cake and send her some on the plate. A lot of cake she'll get from me now! She'll have to come and beg my pardon before I ever say hello to her again. I hate her. "Fat, lazy housewife" she called me, yelling it out for the whole neighborhood to hear. We've been neighbors for ten years but that's the end of things between us. I won't forgive her, and I won't apologize for my boys, either. I hope they break another one of her dahlias! I do!

(She sits down.)

ALL: *(with bowed heads)*: Forgive us our trespasses as we forgive those who trespass against us.

MR. HARRIS *(rising)*: It's all my brother's fault. He talked Mother into it. Imagine my being left only half as much as he was in the will. And the simpering way that Bill's wife said, "I hope you understand." I understand all right. They had Mother in the house with them for three years, and they turned her against me.

Of course, they *did* take care of her when Katie wouldn't stand for her living with us. It's partly Katie's fault. But Mother earned her keep, baby-sitting and sewing. She probably saved Bill more money than he spent on her.

Maybe I am blaming Bill too much. Mother always was soft on Bill, just because he was the youngest. The rest of the family never has a chance when there's a baby in the house. I suppose they worked that will out between them—Mom and Bill. At least they could have told me what they were up to. I felt like a fool at that lawyer's office, being told that I was only getting half as much as Bill.

Of course, she didn't have much money left. I'll bet she'd spent a lot of it on Bill already. He probably got *more* than twice as much as I did. And he keeps smiling like a hypocrite and saying he hopes there's no hard feelings. Even offered the other day to give up part of his share—as if I'd take charity from him. Well, I hope the money rots in his pockets. I'll have nothing more to do with him, even if he is my brother. I won't forgive him. I'll remember this as long as I live.

(He sits down.)

ALL *(with bowed heads)*: Forgive us our trespasses as we forgive those who trespass against us.

MRS. CAREY *(rising)*: That Mr. Jones! I still can't get over the way he treated me. I've bought groceries there for three years and then I bring one thing back and he acts like I was trying to cheat him. The crackers were *stale* and I *told* him so. Of course, we *had* eaten about half of them, but how would you find out if they were stale if you didn't try them? *(Mimicking)* "Mrs. Carey," he said, "you realize that we aren't in business for our health. We have to make a profit and we can't do it if people take advantage of us." Me, take advantage of him! It's the other way around, I'm sure. I've probably bought his thumb a dozen times when he weighed up the meat. And I've never been sure about that girl at the cash register. Probably ups the prices when I'm not looking.

Of course, Mr. Jones *did* deliver my groceries when I was sick. Brought them out himself and even sent me flowers one time. Oh, but that was just to keep my business. It's all money with those fellows. Well, he won't get any more business from me, I can tell you. He was rude and impertinent, and I won't forgive him. There are other places where I can buy my groceries. He'll find out that he lost more than the price of a box of crackers when he got fresh with me.

(She sits down.)

All *(with bowed heads)*: Forgive us our trespasses as we forgive those who trespass against us.

Mrs. Woody *(rising)*: To think that a preacher would talk that way to me! Told me to mind my own business. Of course, he didn't exactly say that. But when I asked him whether Susan was really going to leave her husband, he got real stern and lectured me about gossiping. Everybody knows that I don't gossip. I'm just interested in people, that's all. And that's what we're supposed to be—interested in one another.

I'm sure Susan is going to leave him, though. At least they didn't look any too friendly when they were in church last Sunday. You could have driven a bus between them, the way they were sitting in the pew.

It's the pastor I'm stirred up about, though. Seems to me he's starting to feel pretty important. He forgets that our family have always been good contributors to this church—Ed and his brother and my father and brother. I don't suppose I can get Ed to stop coming to church here. He'll tell me that the pastor was right and that I shouldn't have stuck my nose in in the first place. These men all hang together. But I'm going to quit the women's group. And I'm not going to forget what the pastor said to me. He'll learn that it doesn't pay to get high and mighty with me. I won't forgive him.

(She sits down. The next lines may be spoken by the characters as indicated or by others if additional characters are used in the scene. The lines should build to a climax.)

MR. HARRIS: It's so hard to forgive.

MRS. STONELAND: People are always stepping on you.

MRS. WOODY: It may even do people harm to forgive them.

MR. HARRIS: Just makes them do the same thing again.

MRS. CAREY: People have to be taught a lesson.

MRS. WOODY: I may seem calm outside, but inside I'm full of hatred.

MR. HARRIS: I won't forgive.

MRS. STONELAND: I won't forgive.

MRS. CAREY: Make them suffer.

MRS. WOODY: Just the way they made me suffer.

(A pause, then with bowed heads)

ALL: Forgive us our trespasses as we forgive those who trespass against us.

(Blackout. Then a voice out of the darkness.)

VOICE: Father, forgive them; for they know not what they do.

The Sermon

"Father, forgive them; for they know not what they do." Luke 23:34.

"It's so hard to forgive." All of us would agree with that statement. It makes no difference whether the offense is serious or trivial; forgiveness is difficult. Someone may have called us an unpleasant name or scolded our children for trespassing or cheated us in a business deal or done us great bodily injury. It's all one. The heart of man is always more quickly moved to revenge than forgiveness.

Just because men find forgiveness so difficult, they have always been astonished at the first words of Jesus from the cross. Someone has called this opening statement a greater miracle than all the healings Jesus performed. Certainly there was nothing in the occasion that called for forgiveness. Jesus had been treacherously arrested, found guilty by a kangaroo court, condemned by a judge who thought him innocent, brutally beaten, and then nailed to a cross, a most agonizing method of punishment. Yet under such circumstances he could still say, "Father, forgive them; for they know not what they do."

Astonishing words, but astonishment is not enough. These words are important only when we realize that they are also directed to us. We must never forget that the whole life of Jesus is a parable, an extended illustration. Every word he spoke and everything he did has meaning for each new generation of the church. The forgiveness that Christ extended to his tormentors reaches across the ages and touches our lives. The first word from the cross does not stop at Calvary—it says plainly that our Lord forgives all men, even today.

Of course, we don't need this story to tell us that. The word from the cross is simply the highlight, the dramatic event which underscores the meaning of the whole life of Christ. From the beginning he made it plain that he had come to offer men forgiveness. He declared that he had come to seek and to save sinners. He offered forgiveness to a woman taken in adultery, to tax collectors, to open sinners, to all who came seeking his aid. In perhaps his greatest parable Jesus told the story of a wayward son who came back home, full of sin and bitter memories, and was received in forgiveness by his waiting father. Everywhere in the gospels Jesus is pictured as witnessing to the same truth—our Lord forgives all men.

At this point many preachers are tempted to indulge in a kind of curious logic, a strange application of the text. In order to involve us in the story they often say that all of us have betrayed Jesus, that all of us have condemned him, that all of us have nailed him to the cross. Such "preacher talk" convinces nobody and gains nothing. Not everyone in Jesus' day cried out, "Crucify him, crucify him!" Why should we all be placed under a blanket indictment today? The point should be that if Jesus could pray for those who mistreated him, if he could forgive even his executioners, then there is hope for you and me and for all of sinful mankind. Here we can apply a rule from mathematics: the greater always includes the lesser.

If Jesus prayed for his enemies at the cross, then he has prayed for us as well.

Strangely enough, we need that reassurance, for we never seem to believe in the forgiveness of sins; we never seem to accept God's grace. Think what happens each Sunday morning in the service of worship. In the Lutheran Church the preacher announces: "Almighty God, our heavenly Father, hath had mercy upon us, and hath given his only Son to die for us, and for his sake forgiveth all our sins." In other denominations a similar absolution is used. And yet when the service is over, most people pick up their sins and regrets and worries and walk out with them again, still burdened in heart and conscience. Martin Luther declared in his catechism: "The Holy Spirit day after day forgives my sins and the sins of all believers." And yet Christians often let their guilt pile up so high that they finally have to go to a psychiatrist or write to Ann Landers or find another secular outlet for a troubled conscience. We are like a prisoner who heard the words of a pardon read to him and then shuffled back into the prison line and back into his cell.

Perhaps we hold onto our guilt because we find it so hard to forgive others. Perhaps we are like the characters in the play who talked about forgiveness but were unwilling to forgive. We need to listen to these words from the cross: "Father, forgive them; for they know not what they do." Here we are assured that we have a forgiving Lord. And we must remind ourselves that his forgiveness didn't stop at the cross but reaches down and touches our life too.

And don't choke over those words: "for they know not what they do." Some have insisted that the Jewish leaders and the soldiers could be forgiven because they acted in ignorance, but that we cannot be forgiven because we sin willfully. Don't be misled. There is willfulness in all sin, but there is always ignorance as well. No man ever knows the terrible nature of sin until he is involved in it. The murderer cannot calculate the effect of his act. The liar cannot foresee the result of his lie. Sin is always ignorance, always rebellion.

Thank God there is a Savior who understands, who never lets his hurt and disappointment at our stupidity keep him from reaching out his arms to forgive us. The same Christ who cried from the cross for his tormentors now stands at the throne of grace, bearing in his body the marks of the crucifixion. And still he cries: "Father, forgive them; for they know not what they do."

Now let us place a second picture beside that of our text. It is also the picture of a man facing death. His name is Stephen, and his story is written in the early part of the Book of Acts. Stephen died for his faith in the Jesus who was crucified on Calvary. Listen to his words: "Lord, do not hold this sin against them." Here is the same astonishing cry. Where did Stephen get this spirit? From the one who uttered the first word from the cross. You see, Jesus had let loose his forgiving Spirit in the world. His forgiveness never stops because it is planted in the heart of each believer.

Jesus himself made it plain that this spirit of forgiveness should characterize all his followers. He imbedded his desire for men in the model prayer he gave to his disciples: "Forgive us our trespasses as we forgive those who trespass against us." Jesus gave the church the parable of the unforgiving debtor to impress upon men that there can be no forgiveness of sin unless men are willing to forgive one another. He informed Simon Peter that he was to forgive his brother seventy times seven. Of course he meant that forgiveness was to have no limits.

Wherever men have taken their Christian faith seriously, Christ's spirit of forgiveness has been found. Perhaps it has even been the most consistent mark of a Christian. Yet it is also the place where too many have fallen short. Just like the characters in our play, we can easily pray the Lord's Prayer and still harbor resentment in our hearts toward others. How easy it is for Christian people to magnify small insults and conduct themselves just like their pagan brothers. Leslie Weatherhead in his study of the parables, *In Quest of a Kingdom,* describes how a member of his church said of a fellow member, "I would never have that woman in my house." Weatherhead, who had just become the pastor, replied: "You have been listening to Mr. So-and-So every Sunday for years and years, and yet your idea of Christianity is that you will not have another fellow member of the church, another fellow communicant, in your house. Yet you expect one day that Christ will welcome you into *his* house."[1] The rebuke was well deserved. What a sad thing it is when Christians let bitterness and hatred dwell in their hearts.

Fortunately it isn't always that way. Many Christians have learned the way of Christ, have kept alive his spirit of forgiveness by wiping the slate clean of their resentment. Dr. Clarence Macartney tells of the young Armenian girl who saw her brother killed by a Turkish soldier. Years later, when the girl had become a nurse, she was given the task of nursing this same soldier, now wounded. She cared tenderly for him, and at last he asked her how she could do it, knowing that he had killed her brother. She replied: "I have a religion that teaches me to forgive." Exactly. The basic ingredient in our faith is forgiveness, the forgiveness which God gives to man. But we must keep that forgiveness alive. It must never end.

We are entering the Lenten season. These weeks are a time of preparation for the glorious news of Easter. I can think of no better way to prepare for that season than by purging our hearts of all bitterness. Look deep within and see if you are harboring an unforgiving spirit against any man. See if there is resentment against any person, any fellow Christian, any member of your household. If there is, then ask Jesus Christ to teach you to forgive. Get rid of the petty hatreds of life. Replace them by the spirit of forgiveness.

The biographer of Joseph Stalin said that the Russian leader never forgot or forgave an injury. He always bided his time and, in the end, struck back. Contrast that with the first word of Jesus from the cross: "Father, forgive them; for they know not what they do." Which man do you follow?

"Truly, I say to you, today you will be with me in Paradise."

Luke 23:43

The Second Word

The Power That Doesn't Falter

The Drama

THE CHARACTERS

MR. SWARTZ—a wealthy business man

MR. WINTHROP—the town banker

MR. ANDREWS—meek, middle-aged

MRS. ANDREWS—large, domineering

MISS FAIRVIEW—aristocratic, middle-aged

THE SETTING

The Andrews living room. Five chairs are needed; other furniture can be added. Mr. Winthrop's chair should be set off at stage right or left so that he can talk to the others as a group. All are present and seated at the opening of the play except Miss Fairview.

MR. SWARTZ: Is everyone here?

MR. WINTHROP: No, I invited Miss Fairview too.

MR. SWARTZ: Of course. You wouldn't dare omit her.

MR. WINTHROP: No, although sometimes her ideas aren't exactly sound.

MRS. ANDREWS: I believe she's coming now. Yes, there she is. Come in, Mona dear.

MISS FAIRVIEW *(at door)*: Thank you, Beverly. Hello, everyone. *(All rise; general greetings.)* Pardon me for being late. But of course I'm always late.

MR. WINTHROP: We rather counted on it, Mona. But if you'll all sit down, I'll explain why I called this meeting.

(All are seated except Winthrop. Miss Fairview is farthest from Winthrop.)

MR. SWARTZ: We're waiting to hear from you, J.W.

MR. WINTHROP: Yes, well, I called you people together as an unofficial committee of Trinity Church.

MISS FAIRVIEW *(mockingly)*: Oh, jolly. I never served on an unofficial committee before.

MR. WINTHROP: Hmm. I suppose "committee" is too strong a word, but I felt I needed your advice and backing.

MRS. ANDREWS *(gushingly)*: You know you have our backing, John. Anything John Winthrop sets his approval on has my backing. And my husband's. Isn't that right, dear?

MR. ANDREWS: Yes, Beverly.

MR. WINTHROP: I appreciate your confidence, but first hear what I have to say. I called you people together, not only because you're my friends, but also because you represent the leadership of Trinity Church. Over the past one hundred years, some member of one of our families has been in charge of the affairs of the church almost continually.

MISS FAIRVIEW *(needling)*: Now John, once in a while an outsider has gotten control. Like the late Mr. Barnes, to mention one.

MR. WINTHROP *(pained)*: I know. But the church has always had to turn to our families in time of crisis.

We've supplied the leadership and the money that has built up Trinity Church.

MR. SWARTZ: Especially the money. Seems like these appeals get more frequent and fervent every year.

MR. WINTHROP: We have to do our part, Carl. But this meeting isn't primarily about money. The truth of the matter is that Trinity congregation is threatened with disaster.

MRS. ANDREWS *(jumping up)*: Disaster! Are they going to build that new freeway right through our building, after all the pressure we put on the governor?

MR. WINTHROP: No, no, no. The freeway will go where we said it should go. *(Mrs. Andrews sits down.)* Please let me tell my story and then you can ask questions.

MISS FAIRVIEW: The floor's yours, John.

MR. WINTHROP: Thank you. I'm sure you all know that the area east of our church has changed for the worse during the past ten years.

MISS FAIRVIEW: You mean the Flats.

MR. WINTHROP: Yes, if we must give them that name. All kinds of people have been moving in there. We've all deplored it and even tried to get the city to zone against undesirables, but to no avail. The prominent families in this town don't control the vote as we once did.

MISS FAIRVIEW: Only the governor.

MR. WINTHROP: Mona! Be that as it may, people have moved into the so-called Flats who are poor, uneducated, and even criminal.

Mr. Swartz: It's a disgrace. Something should be done.

Mr. Winthrop: Our pastor agrees with you, Carl. He's proposing that our church make a canvass of the entire area.

Mrs. Andrews: Oh, how wonderful. We can start a mission there and run rummage sales to help the people and maybe even have a charity ball for them. Harold and I will be glad to help. Won't we, dear?

Mr. Andrews: Yes, Beverly.

Mr. Winthrop: I'm afraid you don't understand. What's being proposed is that we canvass the area house to house, and then invite these people to attend and to *join* Trinity Church.

(Shocked silence for a minute)

Mr. Andrews *(struggling to his feet)*: You mean the people from the Flats? Members of Trinity Church? Is that what Rev. Gerald is suggesting?

Mr. Winthrop: He's more than suggesting. He's got his program all worked out and has a lot of members in favor of it. *(Mr. Andrews sinks back into his chair.)* I haven't been in church for a few Sundays, and I just got wind of this business last night. The pastor is going to talk to the vestry about his plan for an all-out evangelism program in the Flats this Friday, and he'll get approval unless something is done to stop him.

Miss Fairview: And you think something should be done to stop him? Is that it, John?

Mr. Winthrop: Of course I do. The founders of Trinity Church didn't envision a church serving the kind of people that live in the Flats.

MISS FAIRVIEW: I'm not so sure about that. I'm not even sure that one hundred years ago the Winthrops and Fairviews and the rest weren't the same kind of people as those who now live in the Flats.

MR. SWARTZ: But Mona, regardless of the past, the people in the Flats aren't our kind of people now. They won't feel at home in our midst. I don't understand what the pastor is thinking about. The whole plan's absurd.

MR. WINTHROP: I'm afraid you underestimate Rev. Gerald. When I pointed that out to him over the phone this morning, he insisted that it was our business to make them feel at home, even if the rest of us had to come to church in our old clothes. He felt that we would be failures as Christians if we didn't win and serve these people.

MISS FAIRVIEW: The pastor knows his way around. I suspect he's got the Christian religion on his side.

MRS. ANDREWS: Well, he doesn't have me on his side. Such foolishness. Things are going well at Trinity. Why doesn't he leave well enough alone? I'm sure Rev. Carver would never have proposed such a plan.

MR. WINTHROP: Unfortunately, Rev. Carver isn't our minister any more. And things aren't going too well at the church, either. Our membership and our attendance are on the decline. When you omit the Flats area, we don't have too many to draw from. That's the appeal of the pastor's plan. Besides, Rev.

Gerald is in line with the whole tenor of the times. *(Bitterly)* The church is getting mixed up in civil rights and church renewal and all sorts of things that we didn't have to face in the past. I suppose we do have to face them now. But we don't have to do it Rev. Gerald's way.

MR. ANDREWS: You sound like you have a plan, John. Do you?

MR. WINTHROP: Of course I have a plan. I wouldn't have called this meeting if I didn't have some solution to offer. It's going to cost money, and it means we'll all have to stick together. But it will work. *(Sits down.)*

MISS FAIRVIEW: Now you sound like John Winthrop, the stony-hearted banker.

MR. WINTHROP: Call me what you will. I'm proposing first of all that we move Trinity Church to a new location.

MR. ANDREWS: Move our church! Where the Andrews family has worshiped for a hundred years!

MR. SWARTZ: That's a hard proposal, John.

MR. WINTHROP: I know, I know. I'll hate it as much as the rest of you. But we've all moved out of that area long ago. It would be a great deal more convenient to have our church in Brentwood Acres, and there are people there that we could serve. Our kind of people.

MRS. ANDREWS: I do know some nice families in Brentwood, the Johnsons and the Kuhlmans and . . .

MR. WINTHROP: Later, Beverly. There's more to my plan. We don't dare leave the area where Trinity's located without a church. The pastor wouldn't stand for that, and he could get lots of support. So I'm proposing that we start that mission that Beverly was talking about. The present Trinity Church building can become the new church for the Flats. That way we'll show our interest in those people and still keep Trinity congregation the way it is now.

MR. SWARTZ: Very clever, very clever, John. But don't you think the Reverend will see through all this and put his foot down? He's no fool, you know.

MR. WINTHROP: I'm aware of that. If the seminaries would only turn out fools for preachers, life would be simpler for us laymen. But some smart ones slip through now and then. Nevertheless, I think we can handle any objection. I'm proposing to this group that we agree on the relocation and then make it plain to the pastor and the vestry that we'll cut off our contributions unless the move is made.

MISS FAIRVIEW: Cut off our contributions! Why that would virtually bankrupt the church. Our four families have been the leading contributors for years.

MR. WINTHROP: Exactly. I think we'll find that money still talks. If the members of Trinity want a new church in a new location, we're willing to pay. If they want to stay where they are and try to win people from the Flats, they'll have to pay.

MISS FAIRVIEW: I can't say much for the Christianity of your plan. But it sounds like it might work.

MR. WINTHROP: It will work. And you needn't go

pious on me, Mona. You don't like the prospect of going to church with people from the Flats any more than I do.

MISS FAIRVIEW: Unfortunately you know I've always been a snob; I suppose it's too late to change now. You win, John.

MR. WINTHROP: What about the rest of you? Carl, can I count on you?

MR. SWARTZ: I suppose it's the only way. I may have to miss that trip to Bermuda this winter on account of this, but a man has to make some sacrifices for his religion.

MR. WINTHROP: And Harold?

MR. ANDREWS: Well—well—I guess so.

MRS. ANDREWS *(jumping up)*: Of course, we agree. I try to be as broad-minded as the next, but the prospect of sitting in a pew beside some of those people who live east of the church is more than I can stand. Just think, if Rev. Gerald's plan should go through, some morning in church we might be sitting right next to a tramp or a drunkard or even a thief.

(Blackout. Then a voice out of the darkness.)

VOICE: Truly I say to you, today you will be with me in Paradise.

The Sermon

"Truly, I say to you, today you will be with me in Paradise." Luke 23:43.

The thief on the cross has always been a source of controversy in the church. To some he is a kind of freak, a man who happened to be in the right place at the right time and who said the right words and got an unexpected trip to heaven. To others the thief is a symbol of the very essence of Christianity, the embodiment of Jesus' mission to call sinners to repentance.

Quite frankly, I think that both views miss the whole point of the story, for the second word from the cross is not simply the description of how a thief was saved. Rather, this utterance by Jesus tells the story of a power so strong that even in a time of terrible weakness that power didn't falter. This word shows what Jesus Christ can do even with a worthless scamp like a thief. And in a day when Christianity seems a rather weak religion, when men wring their hands about the power of sin and darkness in the world, when we hear about the strength of Communism and the weakness of the truth, perhaps we need to get a glimpse again of the one who was the strong man of God. Perhaps this controversial story can give us new hope, new heart. At least, let us take a look not at the cross on the right or the left but on the center cross where the powerful man hung.

Perhaps it was not by chance that Jesus' cross was

placed in the center. At least there is something very symbolic about Jesus' position. For the centrality of the cross testifies to its basic challenge to men. Note that neither of the thieves could ignore this one who hung in their midst. Both of them reviled Jesus for a time before one, somehow touched by the spirit of God, turned to Jesus for help. The thieves should have been so overwhelmed by the agony of their own tortures that they would have had no time for their thorn-crowned companion. Yet they could not ignore this Jesus. Even in the hour of their dying they were drawn by his power and forced to decide, one for and one against a crucified Christ.

What happened to the thieves happened to everyone else who came in contact with Jesus. He called men and they were forced to choose. Matthew, Peter, James, and John heard his call and followed him. The rich young ruler, the people of Nazareth, the Pharisees, and many others heard the call and rejected Jesus. But they all felt the power of this man. Even Pontius Pilate, who thought he could ignore the whole business by washing his hands of it, was forced at last to decide about Christ. The power of Jesus demanded a response from every man he met.

This is what Jesus meant when he declared: "I, when I am lifted up from the earth, will draw all men to myself." John 12:32. This is what he meant when he declared that he had come to cast fire on the earth, or when he prophesied that he would bring division into the very households of men. He has the power to challenge, to attract, and to repel. Thieves felt it. Religious leaders felt it. All men felt the power of this man. Old Simeon was right when he said of Jesus: "Behold, this child is set for the fall and rising of many in Israel, and for a sign that is spoken against." Luke 2:34

And this power has never faltered. Men today aren't any more immune to the Christ than men were back in that first century. Jesus still forces them to decide about him. The world cannot ignore him, cannot forget him, cannot push him aside. The challenge is still: "What do you think of Christ?"

A singular example of this is Communist Russia. The leaders in that land thought that if they educated their young people in atheism, Christianity would wither on the vine as the old people died off. Yet almost forty years after the Russian revolution Russia still faces the challenge of Christ in her land.

We are also witnessing this same persistence of the Christian gospel in our own land. There are men who are busy crying that God is dead, that the church is dead, that we live in a post-Christian era. But somehow the stone never stays on Jesus' tomb. He finds a way to confront men and impels them to decide for or against him. The success of a Billy Graham revival, the tremendously increased interest in Bible study, and the stirring of the social conscience of the church all testify to the power of this man. The words of the hymn are still true:

> Jesus calls us; o'er the tumult
> Of our life's wild, restless sea,
> Day by day his clear voice soundeth
> Saying, "Christian, follow me."
>
> SBH, 553

If only the church were convinced of the compelling power of this Jesus! If only we believed that he attracts or repels all men. Unfortunately we are inclined to limit the gospel, to present it only to those whom we regard as the most likely prospects. We tend to witness only to those who fit our social level. Every Christian worker will confess that he is tempted to classify people into those who are good church material and those who are not. And if he is honest, he will admit that he has often been mistaken on both counts. We don't think that Jesus has an appeal to the down and outer, or to the up and outer (as someone has named the wealthy sinner). With almost godlike assurance we declare of some, "They wouldn't be interested."

If the characters in our play were questioned, they probably would admit to such a bias. Beneath their snobbery is their very real belief that certain people just aren't "religious" and therefore shouldn't be bothered by the church. Such a view is an insult to Jesus Christ. The second word from the cross bears witness to the power of our Lord to challenge *all* men. Admittedly some are harder to reach than others—they may be filled with prejudice against the gospel or resentment against the weaknesses of Christians—but if a hardened criminal dying on a cross could be moved to reach out for help from a crucified Christ, then there is no justification for keeping the gospel from any man. Jesus has power, a power that never falters.

But our Lord represents more than a challenge to man. His is the power that transforms. He does not merely stir our interest—he changes our lives. Look what happened to that thief. One minute a condemned criminal; the next a saved sinner! One minute hanging from a cross; the next residing in Paradise! Talk about rags to riches. The thief certainly knew the meaning of such a transformation, for Jesus

Christ has the power to change, to transform, to save.

This is what Paul meant when he declared: "If any one is in Christ, he is a new creation" (2 Cor. 5:17). This is the point of Jesus' words to Nicodemus about the new birth. It is the point of the opening verses of John's gospel, where we are told that Jesus can give men power to become the sons of God. The witness of Scripture is that Jesus Christ can do things for men that they cannot do for themselves.

The thief is Exhibit A of the power of Jesus to change hearts and lives. This crucified criminal could look back on a wasted life and realize that he was unable to change a single thing he had done. He could atone for none of his shortcomings. He could not even ask forgiveness of those he had wronged, nor seek to make restitution to those he had robbed. He was helpless—as far as his own efforts were concerned he was hopeless. Bishop Hanns Lilje, in his story of his imprisonment by the Nazis, used words that describe the situation of the thief perfectly: "To look back at one's own past gives one a sense of utter helplessness. It is impossible to alter it by a hand's breadth. It is over and done with; yet there it is." [2]

Realizing this helplessness shows us the true meaning of the story of the thief. It is not simply the tale of how a man at the gates of death was snatched into heaven. Instead, we learn here what Jesus Christ can do with a thief: He can make him into a saint. And this thief is simply one among millions who have experienced this strange transforming power of the man on the cross. Jesus made Saul the persecutor into Paul the missionary. He changed Augustine the libertine into Augustine the great Christian leader. Jesus transformed Dwight Moody from a shoe clerk into a great evangelist. He has touched the hearts of savages in New Guinea and South America and Africa and made them into decent, God-centered human beings. The roll call could go on and on.

Admittedly this power is hard to explain. It seems to function when we least expect it. Perhaps that's why the church finds it so hard to believe in the power of our Lord. We think of our own weak efforts to reform ourselves and then find it impossible to believe that the man whose every second word is a curse is a likely prospect for the kingdom of God. We do not think in terms of God's power but in terms of our human weakness.

That's the trouble with the people in our play. They were undoubtedly right in insisting that people from a different level of society would find it hard to mix with them. They were aware that the world is full of drunks and tramps and thieves and that these people aren't beating down the door of the church to get inside. What they overlooked was the transforming power of Jesus Christ, who can take helpless, sinful men and women and change their lives.

Don't misunderstand. The gospel doesn't wipe out all social distinctions. It won't cure a man's bad grammar. Dwight Moody slaughtered the English language to his dying day, even though he was a dedicated Christian. Christ won't change people's taste so that they dress better or act more politely or even smell better because they have become Christians. Some of the inequities, shortcomings, and weaknesses of life remain even after a person has met his Savior.

But the really important part of a human being's existence is changed by the gospel. Jesus Christ makes us all brothers, for we can all become sons of God. He supplies a bond which unites all differences. A bridge cannot eliminate a canyon but it can bring communication between the two sides of the canyon. So Christ bridges our differences when he makes us all citizens of the kingdom of God.

That's the real significance of this story about a saved thief. Christ changed him. Christ touched his heart. Christ took a man who could make no claims, offer no good deeds, or even make any promises for the future, and he made that man a fit candidate for Paradise. This is power, power that never falters, power that can make new men from beaten hulks of humanity.

You see, Christianity is an optimistic religion. Oh, our religion has no illusions about man. It acknowledges man's wickedness and frustration and failure. But our faith says there is a power in the world stronger than all the forces that lead to degradation. We believe in a Savior who, even in his moment of greatest physical weakness, could still attract and transform a thief. We therefore must be optimistic about every soul. We must believe that there is no one beyond the grace of God if he will only turn to Jesus for help. There is nothing wrong with the power of the gospel. We must simply turn it loose in the world.

"Woman, behold thy son!" "Behold thy mother."

John 19:26, 27

The Third Word

The Concern That Never Ceases

The Drama

THE CHARACTERS

MRS. MARTIN—older, rather complacent
MISS SAMPLE—small, sharp-tongued
MRS. DENVERS—young, fashionably dressed
MR. LUKAS—old, rather pathetic

THE SETTING

Corridor or reception room of an old folks' home. Only furniture needed is a table and two chairs. At the opening, Mrs. Martin and Miss Sample are seated at the table. They may be dressed in nurses' uniforms if available.

MRS. MARTIN: Another dreary Sunday.

MISS SAMPLE: These visitors' days always depress me. So few come.

MRS. MARTIN: I know. But when you've been here as long as I have, you'll just accept it.

MISS SAMPLE: I don't think I'll ever accept it. To neglect old people so. It seems children don't have any love for their parents, or at least they don't try to understand what it means to be old and lonely. I'd like to shake some sense into some folks I know.

MRS. MARTIN: You're a real fighter, aren't you? I guess I had your enthusiasm when I was younger.

Now I just try to do my job. The rest isn't any of my business. *(Mrs. Denvers enters.)* Oh, here comes Mrs. Denvers. Wonder what she's going to complain about? Hello, Mrs. Denvers. *(Mrs. Martin and Miss Sample stand up.)*

MRS. DENVERS: Hello, Mrs. Martin. Hello, Miss Sample. Or rather, I guess I should say, goodbye. I think I'll be running on now.

MISS SAMPLE: Why, Mrs. Denvers, you just got here about ten minutes ago. At least I thought I saw you coming in then.

MRS. DENVERS *(embarrassed):* Well, yes, I guess that's about right. But Mother seemed rather tired today, so I didn't want to wear her out. Besides, I have an appointment to play golf with a friend a little later this afternoon.

MRS. MARTIN: You think your mother isn't feeling well?

MRS. DENVERS: Oh, no, no. I'm sure she's all right, and I know you people give her the best of care. It's just that when you reach her age life itself seems a little tiresome, I suppose.

MISS SAMPLE: She always looks forward to your visits.

MRS. DENVERS: I suppose she does. Well, I must be running.

MRS. MARTIN: We'll see you next Sunday, then?

MRS. DENVERS: No, not next Sunday. I have to attend a party my husband's employer is giving. It's in the evening, but it does take a while to get dressed and ready for an event like that. And I'm not sure that

I can come the following week. But I'll be here real soon. Goodbye.

MRS. MARTIN: Goodbye.

MISS SAMPLE: Goodbye.

(Mrs. Denvers exits. Mrs. Martin sits down, Miss Sample walks and talks.)

MISS SAMPLE: I'll bet she'll be here real soon. Her mother's been talking all week about her daughter coming, and she stays ten minutes.

MRS. MARTIN: Remember, she said her mother looked tired.

MISS SAMPLE: Tired! Her mother hasn't anything to do but rest. She's just tired of being left here with no one from her family to take any interest in her, that's all. I'd like to give that Mrs. Denvers a piece of my mind. And Mrs. Denvers' mother isn't the only one. There's Number 9 with no visit for two months from her son or daughter. And Number 11 just fading into the wallpaper because she doesn't even get a letter from her rich children. They're willing to pay us so their mother won't be around to bother them. And Number 14 . . .

MRS. MARTIN: Take it easy, take it easy. You're getting yourself all worked up over nothing. You're not going to change things by making speeches. Just remind yourself of what a nice place this is for old people to spend their last years.

MISS SAMPLE *(sitting down)*: I suppose you're right. But it all seems so cold, so heartless, and it could be so much better if people would only show that they cared.

MRS. MARTIN: Shh. Here comes Mr. Lukas. *(Standing up)* Hello, Mr. Lukas. Going out for a walk? It's not too nice a day for being outside.

MR. LUKAS: Oh, I wasn't going out. But I thought I'd take a look to see if my son might be coming.

MISS SAMPLE: Are you expecting him to visit you today?

MR. LUKAS: Well, I'm not exactly expecting him. But I keep hoping, I keep hoping. 'Course I know he's busy. My son's a very successful lawyer, you know. Mom and me put him through law school even though neither of us finished high school. And he made good. Had the right stuff in him.

MRS. MARTIN: I'm sure he did, Mr. Lukas.

MR. LUKAS: Yes sir. He's one of the best lawyers in the country. Only—only—he never has time to come and see me. You'd think he'd have time once in a while, wouldn't you?

MISS SAMPLE: Yes, you would!

MRS. MARTIN: Now, Miss Sample, it's not for us to say.

MR. LUKAS: No, you two don't know what it's like to raise a boy and then see him grow away from you. I guess different generations just don't go together. But there are some people here whose families visit them. I guess Mom and me didn't do what we should have for John. Somehow we failed to make him feel he was part of a family. Well, this is a nice place to be, a nice place to come to die. I know John isn't coming to see me today. I just fool myself when I come to the door and look for him. Guess I'll go back and lie down for a while.

MRS. MARTIN *(concerned)*: Anything we can do for you?

MR. LUKAS: No, I guess not. It won't be long before visiting hours are over. I always feel better then. *(Exit.)*

MISS SAMPLE *(indignantly)*: Oh, oh, if I could just get my hands on some people!

MRS. MARTIN: Now, now. That wouldn't do any good. Children just have a way of forgetting about their parents, that's all.

MISS SAMPLE: But it would take so little to make these people happy.

MRS. MARTIN: That's just the difficulty. It's the little things that are the hardest to do. Being a hero or a martyr isn't so difficult. But showing love and concern for others—that's where we human beings fail. My, I sound like a preacher. Let's get busy on these records. *(Sits down.)*

MISS SAMPLE: All right. But it would be nice, just once, to meet someone who really showed love and concern for others.

(Blackout. Then the voice:)

VOICE: Woman, behold your son. Behold your mother.

The Sermon

"Woman, behold thy son!" "Behold thy mother." John 19:26, 27.

The third word from the cross is totally normal, totally expected. We would be amazed if Jesus had *not* shown concern for Mary. One does not have to be a Christian, much less the Son of God, to be interested in the welfare of a mother. If this third utterance only tells us how Jesus provided for his mother when he was close to death, the story deserves passing notice, nothing more.

Seen in proper perspective, however, the third word represents an entire dimension of Jesus' life. His whole ministry emphasized that important word "concern." When people brought him the sick, the lame, the blind, Jesus was concerned. When men came with hearts filled with sin or with minds confused by problems, Jesus was concerned. He talked to a Samaritan woman, he visited with a ruler of the Jews who came under cover of darkness, he ate with publicans and sinners. The concern which Jesus showed for his mother was simply a part of a larger concern, his concern for all men. His very presence on this earth was a witness to his interest in the welfare of all.

In some ways, this is the very essence of the good news of the gospel—this matter of concern. Men have lost this feeling for one another. Life goes on at a merry clip, and there's little time for stopping to think about the needs of others. I can remember very clearly an incident which a resident of Chicago described to me. She was hurrying to work one morning and when she came to the steps leading up to the Elevated platform she saw a man stretched across the steps. He was sick or drunk or dead. Nobody bothered to stop to find out, they simply stepped over his prostrate body and hurried on. They weren't concerned.

Somehow we have gotten the notion that God is also like that. We have learned about the vastness of space, stretching away forever. We live on a tiny planet and we are only one among some three billion little vermin crawling on that globe. We feel dwarfed, puny, forgotten. But here comes the message: Jesus is concerned about us. This Jesus who in his hour of agony paid attention to his mother's welfare illustrated by that act his interest in all mankind. Despite our weakness, despite our sin, the Bible reminds us that the Son of God loves us and seeks our best interests.

One of the most moving lines in English literature is that spoken by the mayor of Casterbridge in Thomas Hardy's novel of the same name. Driven by remorse, the mayor attempts suicide, but he is providentially prevented from that act. He says, "Who is such a reprobate as I. And yet it seems that even I be in somebody's hand." [3] That's the witness of the Word of God—we are in somebody's hand. God cares for us. The very hairs of our head are numbered. This concern of Jesus never ceases; it reaches out from the cross to embrace all men. No matter how great the population of the world may become, no matter how vast this universe may be, the Ruler of all things is concerned about man. God's living illustration, Jesus Christ, bears witness to that fact.

It is not wise, I know, to direct a text to one section of a congregation to the exclusion of others. Nevertheless, there is an aspect of this third word that dare not be overlooked. The concern of Jesus for his mother was concern for one who was weak and in many ways defenseless. We don't know Mary's age, but in that day any woman would be helpless without someone to take care of her. Thus when Jesus speaks to his mother, he is also expressing God's concern for the weak, the helpless, the defenseless of this world. At this word, the children, the old, the handicapped, all who find life hard and merciless can take heart.

I know that sometimes men say Christianity is a religion only for the weak, for women and children. I had a man tell me once that religion was a good thing for criminals and women, and the handicapped, but not for real men. That isn't completely so, though it's partly true. For the message of the gospel says that God is especially concerned about those who have no one else to be concerned about them. The Beatitudes talk about the meek, the poor in spirit, and those that mourn. Jesus sends forth his call to those who labor and are heavy-laden. As we think of the tear-stained face of Mary, it should remind us of our Lord's love for every tear-stained face, every weak and mistreated human being.

But this is a double word from the cross. We must not forget that Jesus also said: "Behold thy mother" to his disciple John. Jesus was concerned about Mary, but he discharged that concern through another human being. You see, there's nothing magical about this. God doesn't send angels to take care of old people or to watch over the weak ones in life. He expects that those who are able will bear the burdens of those who need help and assistance. We cannot simply say, "If God cares for the poor, let him get on with it," for we are involved in God's love and care. Perhaps our theme shouldn't be *The Concern That Doesn't Cease* but rather *The Concern That Mustn't Cease.*

The church understood this from the very beginning. Tradition tells us that John took care of Mary as long as she lived; he felt a responsibility for her. But there were soon other widows in the church who needed help, others who required aid and assistance. So the church at Jerusalem began its work of helping others. We are told that some members sold their property and shared a common purse so that the needy might be helped. Later Christians showed concern for children who had been exposed to die by their parents. We find Christians establishing hospitals for those who needed medical treatment. The whole concept of charity and deeds of love had its origin in the feeling that the church must manifest the same concern for all men that Jesus showed.

Sometimes we hear people say, rather harshly, that it is the business of the church to preach the gospel. By this they mean that Christianity shouldn't get itself involved in the physical needs of people or the problems of poverty in a community. The church should stress only "spiritual" things. Such people have never really read the New Testament, for from the very beginning the church was interested in the whole man. Just as Jesus showed love for the helpless and the hopeless, so the church made deeds of charity an essential part of its program from the very beginning.

Once again our subject can be narrowed a little. There is one area where there is special need for concern in our modern world. Our play emphasized that area: the world of the old. We live in a society in which people are living longer than they ever have before; we not only have more teenagers but more oldsters too.

Sometimes the declining years of life are extremely difficult ones. Old people become bitter because they feel neglected. Their friends die and their children seem to forget. We can understand the anguish of the woman in a home who was given a gift and cried: "I don't want gifts. I want people." And perhaps part of the tragedy is that so often people have not properly prepared themselves for the inevitable problems of the aging. As someone said the other day, "You grow old only once. You have no chance to correct your mistakes and try again."

Surely here is a place where we need to follow the example of our Lord in caring for those who are old and have been buffeted by life. Sometimes these people feel a sword through their hearts just as Mary did. Jesus showed us how it is done. He didn't tell John to care for everybody. He told him to care for Mary. This is a one-to-one relationship, a person-to-person action. I like the sentiment expressed by Lady Glencora in one of Anthony Trollope's novels: "If I see a hungry woman, I can give her money; or if she be a sick woman, I can nurse her; . . . but I cannot take up poverty or crime in the lump." [4] The point is that no one asks you to care for people in the lump. In fact, it can't be done that way.

But there are people in your community, perhaps in your congregation, who are lonely, bitter, in need of the interest and concern of their fellow Christians. Jesus has shown the way. You and I need to show these people a personal love and interest. After all, James reminds us: "Religion that is pure and undefiled before God and the Father is this: to visit orphans and widows in their affliction, and to keep oneself unstained from the world" (James 1:27).

Concern! It's a beautiful word. It expresses the love that Jesus had for his mother. It speaks the love that God has for us. It reminds us of the love we must have for others. Actually, concern in Christianity is something like a family heirloom. Jesus showed us what it meant at the cross. The church has continued to manifest it down to the present. You and I must make sure that this concern for fellowmen will never cease.

The Fourth Word

"My God, my God,
why hast thou
forsaken me?"
Matthew 27:46

The Question That Never Dies

The Drama

THE CHARACTERS

MR. GORMAN—middle-aged business man

MRS. GORMAN—housewife

MRS. NASEBY—anguished young mother

MR. BENSON—middle-aged druggist

MRS. WARREN—well-dressed, in mourning

THE SETTING

A living room, with at least two chairs. Lamps and other furniture may be added if desired. When the characters from the newspaper stories appear, they may simply step on stage for their speech. If spotlights are available, they can be directed on some characters, while others are blacked out. At opening, Mr. Gorman is seated in chair, reading newspaper. Wife in other chair, perhaps knitting.

MRS. GORMAN: Anything new in the paper tonight, Charles?

MR. GORMAN: Huh?

MRS. GORMAN *(louder):* I said, anything new in the paper tonight?

MR. GORMAN: No, nothing much. The usual list of accidents, calamities, and troubles. Sometimes the paper is so depressing I wonder why I read it at all.

MRS. GORMAN: Some bad accidents today?

MR. GORMAN: The front page is full of them. I don't know why they print them all. But I guess that's the way things are in this world. Oh, oh, listen to this. Father runs over own son.

MRS. GORMAN: How awful!

MR. GORMAN: Yeah, it sure is. Boy darted right out of his mother's arms and under the car wheels while the father was backing the car out of the garage. I suppose the parents will never forgive themselves.

MRS. GORMAN: It's terrible, even to think about it.

(Lights dim; Mrs. Naseby steps into spotlight.)

MRS. NASEBY: It all happened so quickly. One minute he was standing close beside me and the next he was under the wheels. *(Remembering)* Oh! And his father doesn't say anything, he just looks at me with that hurt look in his eyes. That's the worst of it. If he'd only shout at me or call me names or do something, I think I'd feel better. I told him that the boy was all right, out of the way of the car. And he was. He was holding onto my hand and I didn't think he'd try to get away. And then . . .

He always was such a good boy. Minded me in everything. Never had to correct him twice. And I had warned him about getting too close to the car. I don't know what made him dart away from me. I guess he was so anxious to get into the car with his daddy. Jimmy always was daddy's boy. Even when he was a baby, Henry could get him to stop crying when I couldn't do a thing with him. Guess that's why his father sits like that, saying nothing to me.

Why did it have to happen? Why couldn't God

have held him back? Just a few inches and the car would have missed him. What kind of world is it when things like this can happen! We go to church and try to do right. And now our son, our only son, is gone. Why, God, why? Give me back my son. Why couldn't I have died instead? I can't understand. I won't understand! God, show me some kindness! Show me some love! But there isn't any kindness or love for me any more. Why, why did it have to happen? *(Exit.)*

(Spotlight fades out and lights are brought on room again.)

MRS. GORMAN: That poor father and mother. You wonder why things like that have to happen.

MR. GORMAN: Yes, and there are more stories like that in the paper today. Here's the story of a local boy killed fighting the Communists.

MRS. GORMAN: Another one! That makes three this month.

MR. GORMAN: It's beginning to strike home. Fighting doesn't seem so far away when someone from your own community suffers.

MRS. GORMAN: It's always a shock for people when they get a message like that. Everybody knows that people get killed in wars, but you always think it won't happen to your boy.

MR. GORMAN: You can't fight a war without somebody getting hurt.

MRS. GORMAN: That never makes it any easier when it strikes home.

(Lights dim; Mr. Benson steps into spotlight.)

MR. BENSON: Bill! Killed in action. That's what the messenger said. I suppose we'll get more details later, but they're not important. All a man's hopes gone in one little word—dead. I thought Bill would come home some day and take over the drug store when I was ready to retire. Now I suppose one of the chains will buy me out. I don't really care. When a man has only one son to carry on his name and something happens to that son, that's the end of it—the end of dreams and plans. But it isn't really what's going to happen to the drug store that upsets me. It's Bill, Bill. That's what hurts. He was bone of my bone and flesh of my flesh. A chip off the old block, everybody said. He walked like me and talked like me. When we sat in church people said they couldn't tell us apart except for my gray hairs. Church! What does church mean to me now? Why did God let my son be killed? There were plenty of boys there, boys that had no one to love them or to plan on them. Probably some no-good scoundrels, too. Why did the bullet have to strike Bill? What kind of world is it when our young people have to fight and get shot at? Dirty Communists! But I suppose some of them have sons who get killed too. It's not right, not right. Why doesn't God stop this war? Why doesn't somebody do something? Only, even if they did, it's too late for my son. Bill's dead and nothing will bring him back. Why did you let it happen, God? Why? Why? *(Exit.)*

(Spotlight fades out and lights are brought on room again.)

MRS. GORMAN: It's hard to lose a grown son. Hard to make plans and have them all shattered.

MR. GORMAN: Yes. But at least when you get hit by a bullet, it's a quick death and soon over with. Look at this item. That Carl Warren finally died.

MRS. GORMAN: The boy who had leukemia?

MR. GORMAN: That's the one.

MRS. GORMAN: I thought he was getting better. At least there was something in the paper about him a few weeks ago.

MR. GORMAN: Guess they were too optimistic. Anyway, it says that he died last night.

MRS. GORMAN: Oh, dear. What a lot of misery there is in the world.

(Lights dim; Mrs. Warren steps into spotlight.)

MRS. WARREN: I thought there was a chance to save him. He seemed so good for a while. Even the doctors were encouraged. And now—nothing. You bring a boy into the world and nurse him and care for him and make your plans for him, and then some disease comes along, and that's it. We could have given Carl everything—education, clothes, money. And we couldn't even buy him a day of life. What's life all about, anyway? My husband works day after day in that office, writing copy for advertisements. He saves and invests all he can, but for what? Nothing! And to have to see my boy getting weaker every day. He knew he was going to die, and all the rest of us knew it too, only nobody wanted to say anything. Even Pastor Gibbons didn't want to talk about death to Carl for fear it would make him give up. Pastor Gibbons—a lot of good he did us. Oh, yes, he prayed and asked for God's help, but no help came. When Carl started looking better for a little while, I thought maybe there was something to this praying after all. But God didn't hear our prayers. He just let my boy die. Why, God, why? Don't you care? Can't you understand a mother wanting her child to live? What difference would it make to you if one little boy lived a few years more? If you could have saved his life, why didn't you? I don't believe there is any God. No one to hear, no one to answer prayers. I'll never believe again. There's nothing left for me in this world. Nothing! Nothing! *(Exit)*

(Spotlight fades out and lights are brought on room again.)

MR. GORMAN: It's strange that there should be so much suffering in this world. Just seems to be no end to it. A fellow can't help asking, Why?

MRS. GORMAN: I know. We're supposed to go on believing and trusting but it's hard to do sometimes. You just can't understand.

MR. GORMAN: Guess we're not supposed to. Have to leave it all in God's hands. But it makes a person think.

(Blackout. Then the voice.)

VOICE: My God, my God, why hast thou forsaken me?

The Sermon

"My, God, my God, why hast thou forsaken me?"
Matthew 27:46.

A child is killed by a car. A soldier dies on the battlefield. A young man dies after a lingering sickness. And we ask, "Why?" The hurts of this life seem to have no answer. Fate is blind, men say, for she strikes in haphazard fashion. And each time there is pain, sickness, or death we demand to know, "Why?"

A man hangs on a cross writhing in agony. And he too asks the disturbing question: "Why? Why hast thou forsaken me?" We are somewhat shocked to hear these words from Jesus' lips. The only comforting thing is that this is the *fourth* word from the cross. If Jesus had begun his suffering with such a cry, we would wonder. If he had ended his life with such a despairing question, we too would despair. But since this is the fourth word, the middle word of the seven, we can consider it and evaluate it and partially understand it.

Actually this fourth word from the cross has a familiar ring to it. Jesus is really quoting from Psalm 22, where David expressed the agony of his soul. Moreover, the Bible is filled with statements of others who asked God in one way or another the same question: why something had happened. There was Naomi, Ruth's mother-in-law, who asked to be called Mara or "bitter" because "the Almighty has dealt very bitterly with me" (Ruth 1:20). There was Elijah, who was ready to die in the desert because he thought all his efforts for God had resulted in failure. There was Jeremiah in a pit, and Mary and Martha who had lost their brother Lazarus, and a host of others who had experienced misfortune in one way or another. All of these expressed the same thought as Jesus spoke from the cross. Why? Why? This is the question that never dies.

Whenever men have had to face the ugliness that sin has brought on this earth, they have cried out in despair. There is probably not a man or woman reading these words who hasn't felt at some time like Jesus on the cross—forsaken by God. A recent book about Job has the interesting title: *More Than a Man Can Take.* That's what happens to us at times. We face things that seem more than we can take. As one of the characters in our play says, "What a lot of misery there is in this world." How true, and when we experience that misery or sometimes even when we just witness it, we are moved to cry out, to utter the question that never dies: "Why?"

While we would not wish our Lord one moment of agony, there is a certain comfort for us in hearing these words from the lips of Jesus. When he feels forsaken, when he asks why, we feel he is truly one of us. Our Savior is no plaster saint, no aristocrat, shielded from the problems of life. This is a man who has suffered, who has felt man's common problems, who has experienced what we must experience. He was in all manner tempted as we are, the Bible tells us.

Moreover, these words remove our guilty feelings about despair. Somehow we have gotten it into our heads that a true Christian meets all the problems of life with a stoic calm. Man is supposed to trust and never question. "Stiff upper lip," we say, as though this were a heavenly command. But there is nothing in the Bible that demands such an inhuman attitude. After all, Job longed for the day of his death. Jeremiah cried out in despair to God. And Jesus on the cross voices the same attitude: "My God, my God, why hast thou forsaken me?"

I'm not saying that a Christian should rave against God or curse him when things happen that he cannot understand. After all, Jesus still cried to *God* for help. He did not turn his back on his Father. But grief and woe can break the heart of a believer too, so he should not be condemned because he voices his despair. Christianity demands no superhuman effort. It is a religion for beings of flesh and blood who can be hurt and distressed, and who may be moved to ask the question that never dies: "Why?"

I can remember an experience in my parish ministry which illustrates this truth very clearly. A member who had been ill for some time died very suddenly. His wife, because she had loved her husband, was overcome with grief, even though she should have known what was going to happen. But as she grieved, the family became increasingly irritated because she was so upset. They felt her attitude was sinful and unchristian. Finally I had to tell them: "Leave her alone. Her faith will pull her through, but you can't expect more than a questioning 'why' from her right now." She did emerge from that experience stronger in her faith than before, but it was wrong to expect her to shake off her grief and come up smiling the next day.

Let us not forget that our Lord cried out in pain

and agony. He voiced the question that is common to all men, the question that never dies. We do not give thanks that he was driven to utter such a cry. But we can be thankful that the fourth word from the cross was recorded so that we can understand what God expects of man, and so that we can realize that we are not lost souls when we cry out: "Why?"

But I said a moment ago that "our Lord" spoke these words. And that fact forces us to define and redefine our problem. We cannot forget that this despairing Christ is also the one who had declared: "I and the Father are one" (John 10:30). We cannot overlook the fact that this same Jesus also spoke with authority to a thief and insisted: "Today you will be with me in Paradise" (Luke 23:43). This fourth word from the cross may be a question common to all mankind, but what disturbs us here is the *uncommon* cry from the lips of Jesus.

Of course, we will never know the complete story. The relationship between Jesus and the Father is a mystery to us. Here we truly see through a glass darkly. But it is obvious that something strange, mysterious, disturbing, happened at Calvary when the fourth word was uttered. The sun had hidden its light. When the cry came, it welled up out of indescribable agony. Jesus cried with a loud voice.

What was the burden upon that great soul which brought forth such a cry? Sheer physical suffering? Or more than that? The New Testament tells us that God made him who knew no sin to be sin on our behalf. It reminds us that God laid on him the iniquity of us all. Is this the spot where God was letting his Son bear the sins of all mankind? Who can say? But at least we can agree that in some sense

Jesus' suffering came to a climax as he uttered the fourth word. Somehow God was in all this. His Son was drinking the bitter cup. Perhaps the hymn writer has put it best: "But the deepest stroke to wound him was the stroke God's justice gave."

This is not common suffering. This is not the common cry of man. This is the uncommon cry of God's Son, voicing through an age-old question a deeper agony, a deeper cry. These words bring tears to the eyes and terror to the heart when uttered by Jesus. Here is one who is suffering the very pains of hell itself, for that is what hell is, being cut off from God. No wonder Jesus prayed in anguish in the Garden. No wonder he trembled at the thought of drinking such a cup of bitterness.

And yet, despite our sorrow as we listen to this terrible cry, it also brings us a great sense of relief. For a man does not suffer like this willingly unless he is moved by an overwhelming love. Calvary is not the story of a lynching but of a sacrifice. This is a conspiracy, a conspiracy of love. You cannot argue with a man who suffers like this for you. You cannot say, "God, do you love me?" after witnessing God's Son taking the penalty of your sins on the cross.

And here is the connection between the common cry of men and the uncommon cry of Jesus. Men will always be moved to cry, "Why, God, why?" And in this life we will not be able to find any answer to that query, the question that never dies. But one thing we can know—God loves us. After Calvary, after the fourth word from the cross, there should be no doubt of that. We may not be able to explain why a boy dies from leukemia; we may not know why God permits a father's only son to be killed in a war or why

God allows a child to run under a car that his father is backing out of a driveway. But in the face of every trouble we can cling to one truth: God loves man.

Just as a young man, upset by something his girl friend may have said or done, consoles himself with the knowledge of her declared love, so the Christian, unable to grasp all the meanings of life, consoles himself with his realization of God's love. This fourth word from the cross may seem the most mysterious statement ever made by Jesus. Yet it holds the clue to all other mysteries, to all questions that perplex and beset us in time of trouble. God loves. God loves me. The fourth word changes in translation from speaker to hearer. When it leaves Jesus' lips the cry is, "My God, my God, why hast thou forsaken me?" When it reaches our ears it says, "I love you."

"I thirst."

John 19:28

The Fifth Word

The Nature That Doesn't Change

The Drama

THE CHARACTERS

MISS JANICE MERRINGTON—middle-aged, a little sharp-tongued

MRS. HELEN DARNLEY—a widow, middle-aged, more mellow than Janice

MR. ARTHUR MERRINGTON—younger brother of Janice, earnest, concerned

"OLD RAGS" JOHNSON—typical Bowery bum who has seen better days

THE SETTING

A "rescue" type mission. Four chairs are all that is needed, but signs, tables, chairs, etc., may be added.

JANICE: Any sign of Arthur yet?

HELEN *(looking out):* No, Dear. But I'm sure he'll be along any minute now.

JANICE: I am so worried when he's out alone in this part of town. So many terrible things happen. And it's starting to get dark already.

HELEN: Now, Janice, don't get excited. Arthur can take care of himself. Besides, the people in this neighborhood know him now. They won't bother him.

JANICE: I suppose not. Sometimes I wonder why we

ever came to this terrible part of the city to do mission work.

HELEN: We thought the people needed us. Remember?

JANICE: Yes, of course. And I still think they do. These people need the gospel. Only, how do you convince them that they do? You can't help people who don't want to be helped.

HELEN: Maybe we'll learn the answer today. That is, if Arthur is able to find "Old Rags" Johnson.

JANICE: What a name—Old Rags. But I suppose it fits very well. *(Noise outside.)* Do you hear someone?

HELEN: Yes, I think I do.

JANICE *(at door):* It's Arthur. And there's someone with him.

HELEN: Old Rags?

JANICE: I hope so. Come in, Arthur. I'm so glad you're back.

ARTHUR *(chiding):* You've been worrying about me, as usual. You're still big sister, looking after baby brother. Now, Ladies, I'd like you to meet our guest, Mr. Johnson.

JOHNSON: Old Rags Johnson. There's been no Mr. Johnson for twenty-five years.

ARTHUR: Old Rags, then. This is my sister, Miss Janice Merrington, and her friend, Mrs. Helen Darnley.

JOHNSON: Please to meet ya. *(General greetings.)* Where's my four bits?

ARTHUR: Not so fast. I promised you fifty cents if you'd come and talk with us for a little while. Let's all sit down first. *(They are seated.)*

JOHNSON: Don't you preach no sermon at me. I've heard all the sermons I want to hear and I'm still just a bum.

ARTHUR: There'll be no preaching today, Old Rags. In fact, if you can't give us some help, I'm afraid there'll be no preaching at all from us here at the rescue mission. We'll have to close up.

JOHNSON: What's the matter? Runnin' out of dough?

JANICE: Oh, no! We have plenty of money. But nobody comes to our services. Helen can play the piano like a concert artist, Arthur can preach wonderful sermons, and I can sing gospel hymns. But nobody comes. We've tried everything to get a crowd.

HELEN: We've given away soup and coffee and doughnuts. We've offered to find people jobs, we've paid people's rent. We've done everything we know how to do to show that we're concerned about this neighborhood.

ARTHUR: I guess we're a little discouraged, Old Rags. That's why we wanted to talk to you. Everyone says you've been here a long time and know the whole district and the people in it.

JOHNSON: You've come to the right man, anyway. I know every alley and bar twenty-five blocks in any direction. Guess I've slept in all of them. But I don't get it. You say you've got lots of dough. Why don't you go someplace else and enjoy it?

ARTHUR: I suppose it's hard for you to understand. You see, the three of us grew up together. Our families always had money, and we could have anything we wanted.

JANICE: One day we went for a drive through this part of town. And it shocked us.

HELEN: We never knew people lived like this. In flop-houses and tenements.

ARTHUR: We'd read about it, of course, but it's different when you see it.

JANICE: That very day we decided to do something for the people in this neighborhood. We're all Christians, and we wanted to organize a rescue mission. We didn't get much help from our church friends, so we decided to do the work by ourselves.

HELEN: Arthur rented this store front and bought all the supplies. We were really proud the first day we moved in here.

ARTHUR: That was six months ago. And we've had no success. None whatsoever!

JANICE: Mr. Old Rags, what's the trouble? My brother is a good preacher. And we do want to help the people here. But everything we try fails to work.

HELEN: Even when we give someone some money to get on his feet, he just spends it for drink.

JANICE: We're discouraged. It's terrible to be full of love for people and not be able to show that love.

ARTHUR: Can you help us? You know the people in this neighborhood. You know what they think of us. What are we doing wrong? What do they want from us? How can we help?

JOHNSON: I kin give you one piece of advice. Go back where you came from and leave us alone.

HELEN: But why? Why?

JANICE: I don't want to take that for an answer. We have a message about a Savior who died for people like you, Old Rags. There must be some way we can convince people of that.

JOHNSON: There's a way, all right. But there's no use tellin' you about it.

ARTHUR: Tell us. No matter what it costs, we'll try it.

JOHNSON: No matter what it costs, eh? We'll see. But first, let me ask yah a question. Where do you ladies eat your lunch?

JANICE *(surprised):* Why, we bring it.

JOHNSON: You don't eat at any of the joints around here, hah?

HELEN: No, we . . . .

JOHNSON: They're a little greasy, ain't they?

JANICE: Yes, we . . . .

JOHNSON: And there are bugs, too. You can see the cockroaches walkin' round on the floor in most joints in this neighborhood.

ARTHUR: The women . . . .

JOHNSON: You don't need to explain. I once had money to eat in fancy places, before I started drinkin'. It waren't easy, gittin' used to eatin' in some greasy spoon. I don't even see the dirt anymore. Now, suppose yah tell me where you live.

ARTHUR: Over in Park Heights.

JOHNSON: Park Heights. Fancy neighborhood.

JANICE *(defiantly):* We have beautiful homes there, if that's what you want to know.

JOHNSON: I figgered that. Ever think of sellin' and movin' here? Close to the mission?

HELEN: In a tenement?

JOHNSON: Yeah, a tenement. You wouldn't like that, would ya?

JANICE: Well . . . .

JOHNSON: There's rats there. And bedbugs. The halls stink.

HELEN: We know. We've visited some of the people in their homes. It's a disgrace how they have to live. The city ought to clean up this whole section.

JOHNSON: Yeah, the city ought to. But it ain't gonna do it. And you couldn't live in those places the way they are now, could ya?

ARTHUR: It isn't that we couldn't do it. It's just that we've never been used to such places.

JOHNSON: Nope. And you ain't likely to get used to them. And there's the whole business for ya.

JANICE: You mean we can't get anyone to come to our mission because we're strangers, outsiders?

JOHNSON: We're all strangers here, driftin' in and out. But you can't help people if you don't know what things are like for them. Oh, you can see the dirt and disease and smell the stinks. But what do you know about the hopelessness of being poor, the hopelessness of facing every day and knowin' it ain't gonna be any better than the day before?

What do you know about wakin' up each mornin' and wishin' you hadn't. What do you know about hunger as a permanent boarder in the house? That's the trouble. You can't help us because you ain't like us.

ARTHUR: We try hard to understand.

JOHNSON: I know. I'm not sayin' you ain't kind and well-meaning, but there's only one way anybody can help us. He has to be a part of all we live with.

ARTHUR: Maybe we could try it for a time. Maybe we could move into a tenement apartment and live right in this neighborhood.

JOHNSON: No, that wouldn't do. You could always get out if you didn't like it. We can't. If you got rid of all that dough of yours and if you lived here because there wasn't no other place for ya, and then if you still wanted to help us—that might be different.

JANICE: You drive a hard bargain.

JOHNSON: I know. That's why I said it was hopeless. The only guy who could help us would be someone who would give up everything for us. If a man loved people in this neighborhood enough to live here and help us all he could, even if we didn't like it, even if we was mean enough to mistreat him and maybe even kill him, that might make a change here. But that's the only way.

(Blackout. The voice speaks out of the darkness.)

VOICE: I thirst.

The Sermon

"I thirst." John 19:28.

The world was made by him. Every drop of water in the universe owes its origin to him. Every gurgling, rushing mountain stream came from his hands. Every deep, cool well exists because of his work. For as John reminds us: "All things were made through him, and without him was not anything made that was made." John 1:3. And he cried out, "I thirst." Can you think of any greater irony than that? Do you know of any greater paradox? Jesus Christ was thirsty. The Son of God lacked the most common, the most necessary thing in this world—water.

In that very lack we have revealed for us the profound nature of the incarnation, the birth of God's Son as a man. We could ask no finer or more striking proof of Jesus' true humanity than this fifth word from the cross. Unfortunately, many people have felt that this utterance is trivial, unimportant. It is the word most often omitted by preachers. And when men do speak of it, they are inclined to spiritualize it, to speak of Christ thirsting for souls. Of course, he thirsted for souls, all his life. But the meaning of the fifth word from the cross requires no mystical explanation. It says: Jesus Christ was thirsty. The Son of God, the creator of all things, cried out for a drink to ease his parched throat.

That cry should make us realize one simple truth: he became one of us. Jesus Christ breathed the same air that we do. He ate and digested his food as we do. He grew hungry and tired as we do. His throat felt thirst, just as ours does. The needs of the body were his needs too. Here is the picture of a tremendous sacrifice, a terrible surrender, a humiliation as the church often names it. For whether we want to admit it or not, our human nature, our bodies of flesh and blood, limit us. I'm not talking about how we grow sick and die or at least grow old and die. The greater limitation is the one which we feel every day.

How our mind races beyond our body! We start on a trip and we want to reach our destination by continuous travel. But the body says, "No." It says, "I'm tired or hungry or sleepy or thirsty," and we are compelled to take a break and limit our activities. We want to read a book, but our eyes grow tired. We want to walk to our destination but our feet play out. So it goes. A middle-aged man once described what was happening to him when he played tennis. He said: "My mind tells me to rush toward the net, swing my racket with smashing force, and drive the ball into the far corner of the court. Then my body says, 'Who? Me?' " This is the humiliation of the flesh, the restriction which our humanity puts on us.

And all of this Jesus Christ took on himself when he was born in Bethlehem. He became one of us. Somehow that's obvious and yet so hard to believe. We have surrounded Christ with such an aura, we have put so many haloes on his head, we have talked about his miracles and his divinity, until somehow he seems far removed from us. Listen to this fifth word from the cross—I thirst. That cry should jolt us back to reality. These are the words of a real human being, a man feeling the limitations of flesh.

This cry assures us that our Lord was bone of our bone and flesh of our flesh. The same chemicals that make up our body composed his. The same needs, the same problems, troubled his flesh as trouble us.

How much clearer this makes our understanding of God. In Christ we can see God in action. We can learn about him, study him, reflect on his actions and his words. Indeed, this is the only kind of God that men can understand. All the fine reasonings of man, all the philosophical explanations of God, leave us cold. It's not so hard to understand how a man can be an agnostic if we think only in these speculative terms. The "God is dead" advocates have something to say if we are only talking about man-made descriptions of God.

Even the efforts which Christian people make to describe God are very feeble. Think of that beautiful modern hymn by Walter Chalmers Smith. The first verse says:

> Immortal, invisible, God only wise,
> In light inaccessible hid from our eyes,
> Most blessed, most glorious, the Ancient of Days,
> Almighty, victorious, thy great Name we praise.
>
> SBH, 172

There's a marching rhythm to the words. And yet this is a picture of God beyond us, beyond our power to grasp. But a God who became a man, who would die on a cross, who would grow thirsty and cry out in pain—that is a God we can understand. This is why the Bible is filled with so-called anthropomorphisms, descriptions of God in human imagery. The Old Testament speaks about the face of God and the feet of God. Men are inclined to sneer at such childish expressions, yet there is nothing childish in such terms. Man can only grasp a God who partakes of our nature, who is one of us.

And such a God is the only one who can give us a sense that he understands. The figures in our play reflect this truth. Only one who has lived among men, who has shared their burdens and experienced their heartaches can truly win men's hearts. And this must be a real experience, not a sham or a masquerade. Many of the ancient religions pictured the gods as taking on a human form for a short time to mingle with men. But Jesus Christ put himself under the yoke of the flesh. He burned his bridges behind him, he laid aside his glory, and he came and experienced the same troubles that we face. He was not God come slumming in his sinful world. He was one of us.

The poet Louis Untermeyer expresses in "Caliban in the Coal Mines" [5] the same mood as the man in our play. Untermeyer pictures the miners, suffering in the darkness of the mines and then he says,

> God, You don't know what it is—
> You, in Your well-lighted sky—
> Watch the meteor whizz;
> Warm, with the sun always by.

The last stanza is particularly striking:

> Nothing but blackness above
> And nothing that moves but the cars—
> God, if You wish for our love,
> Fling us a handful of stars!

But the story of Calvary is the story of a God who came down and worked in the coal mines, a God who experienced what we experience because he became a human being. As the writer of Hebrews put it: "Since therefore the children share in flesh and blood, he himself likewise partook of the same nature" (Hebrews 2:14a).

But it was a long time ago that Jesus Christ cried, "I thirst." Much has happened since then. This Jesus, we believe, arose from the dead, ascended into heaven, and is seated at the right hand of God. And with this language we are tempted to lose sight of the human nature of Jesus. It's so easy to think of him again as a disembodied spirit, a being far different from us. He has become like a man who once worked in the factory with us but is now promoted to the front office and probably wouldn't recognize or speak to us any more.

Here we must remind ourselves of our theme: "The Nature That Doesn't Change." Jesus Christ became a human being, not just for the thirty-three years he spent in his earthly ministry, but for all time. He is still bone of our bone and flesh of our flesh. The cry "I thirst" is not just an expression of a temporary nature and a temporary inconvenience. The incarnation was for real. Jesus is man, our elder brother, the second Adam, and he remains so for all eternity. Note how carefully Jesus made plain to his disciples that he was the same human Jesus after the resurrection as before. He ate with them. He talked with them. He invited them to touch him and handle him. Those who would make the resurrected Christ some kind of ghost or strange being not of this earth simply refuse to read the record. John corrects such foolish notions in the opening words of his first epistle when he speaks of that "which we have heard, which we have seen with our eyes, which we have looked upon and touched with our hands . . . " (1 John 1:1).

Jesus Christ is just as human today as he was when he walked on this earth. He has gone forward to greater glory, and we are to follow. But his humanity should bring us great joy, for it means that we have a friend in the very courts of heaven. It means that there is someone there who understands our problems, our cares, our weaknesses, for he has been on this earth and still retains his human nature. The man in the slum need not fear that God will not understand his problems. Jesus Christ has been there. The people who mourn, those who wrestle with temptations, those who rejoice, and those who sorrow can all have the assurance that ours is a God who understands. The impressive descriptions of heaven in the Bible may overwhelm and overawe us, but what cause is there for worry? Our brother is there, and his smiling human face will give us courage to march past the thronging cherubim and seraphim to the very throne of God itself.

Sometimes men accuse parts of the church of being "second person unitarians." That is, they say we put too much stress on Jesus Christ and forget God as a Father and God as a Holy Spirit dwelling in man. Perhaps there is some justice to the charge, but this overemphasis is easy to understand. God as creator overawes us with his millions of galaxies and his thundering power. We feel like crying as Job did: "Behold, I am of small account; what shall I answer thee? I lay my hand on my mouth" (Job 40:4). God as Spirit mystifies us. We do not dwell in a realm of spirits. But Jesus Christ became one of us, and his nature has not changed and will not change. He has known hunger and thirst, pain and death. To him every human being, whether slum dweller or rich man, old or young, wise or foolish, can cry, "Jesus, have mercy on me," and be sure of a sympathetic hearing. For such a God we can only echo the words of Isaac Watts:

> Here, Lord, I give myself away;
> 'Tis all that I can do.
>
> SBH, 486

"It is finished."

John 19:30

The Sixth Word

The Ending That Doesn't End

The Drama

THE CHARACTERS

HANS—a successful doctor
FRED—a school teacher, rather bitter
ABEL—a farmer, athletic, sympathetic
MARY—small, sharp-tongued
SUSAN—glamorous, a TV personality

THE SETTING

The group is either seated around a table or on chairs in a semicircle. Hans and Susan on each end, Fred in the center.

HANS: Well, this has been a wonderful class reunion. Too bad some of the rest couldn't make it.

FRED: It's a little disappointing. Only five of us from the class of 1927. I had hoped some more would come.

MARY: We're scattered pretty far and wide, you know.

ABEL: Besides, there aren't too many of us left. Only eighteen out of a class of thirty-five from good old Chatham High.

SUSAN: I suppose we're the tough ones. Still alive and able to travel.

FRED: You certainly are. Especially able to travel. I

don't think we mentioned a place on the globe where you hadn't been.

SUSAN: Don't sound so envious. Every town begins to look like Indianapolis after a while.

FRED *(standing up, after a pause):* I suppose we ought to break this up, even though it's been a pleasant evening.

ABEL *(standing up):* You're probably right. We're getting too old to miss our beauty sleep.

HANS: The evening's young yet. I'm good for a couple more hours. Still, if the rest of you think we should go . . . *(stands up).*

MARY: You men haven't changed a bit. You've finished bragging about your jobs and your homes and your families, and now you're getting bored with one another.

FRED: You haven't changed either, Mary. Always the sharp tongue.

SUSAN: And the correct analysis.

HANS: That, too.

MARY: I knew there'd be a time in the evening chatter when we'd all wonder what to say next. It's hard to pick up the threads after we've been away from each other so long. *(Taking small notebook out of handbag)* So I brought along a little conversation primer that may keep you here longer.

ABEL: Now, what in the world . . . .

MARY: You know I've always been a saver of scraps of paper. I'm the ideal secretary or archivist. My attic's full of letters, school papers, dance programs, and what have you. And the other day while rummaging around I found this *(holds out notebook)*.

HANS: What is it?

MARY: The Class Wish Book.

ABEL: The what?

MARY: The Class Wish Book. Don't you remember how our class met just before graduation at Suttloff's Restaurant for a party?

SUSAN: Of course. And for a lark we all wrote down what our goals and ambitions were. That's the Class Wish Book.

FRED: I remember now. And of course we gave the book to Mary. And she didn't have the courtesy to lose it.

MARY: You know I didn't lose it. I've got it right here. And tonight the skeletons come out of the closet.

HANS: Do you mean you're going to read all that adolescent stuff we wrote?

MARY: Not all of it. But I thought you might be interested in hearing what we intended to do with ourselves and then compare it with the way things turned out. Or would you rather go home now?

FRED: If we had any sense, we'd go home. But you have us hooked, so carry on, Mary. *(The men sit down again.)*

SUSAN: I'm dying to know what some of the rest of you people put down.

HANS: Suppose you read us what you wrote, Mary. That'll be a good starting point.

MARY: All right. Mine's short and sweet. I was going to be a school teacher and teach English literature.

SUSAN: What happened?

MARY: The usual thing. I met a man and got married.

ABEL: That doesn't sound like too bad a substitute for your plans.

MARY: I can't complain. Henry's been good to me. Only—I haven't read a book in five years. And I was the gal who was in love with English literature.

HANS: Ping! Our first illusion gone.

FRED: You don't have to read my story from that book. I know what I put down. I was going to be a big game hunter in Africa. And I became that school teacher in your place, Mary.

MARY: Lucky fellow.

FRED: I hate to disillusion you. But after you've shouted at noisy classes for thirty years and read thousands of themes with misspelled words in almost every sentence, a teacher's life doesn't seem very glamorous. I've read all the books you missed, Mary. But I've had to do it to keep up with my work, and that takes all the joy out of it, let me tell you.

SUSAN: We seem to have hit on an unpleasant subject. Maybe this isn't such a good idea, Mary.

MARY: Cheer up. Better things are ahead. Here's your story, Susan.

SUSAN: O me! What did I write?

MARY: You should remember. Susan said that she

wanted a little cottage with a picket fence, three kids, and a husband who came home from work at five each night. Isn't that something! And she ends up as a glamorous radio and TV personality who travels around the world at the drop of a rumor.

FRED *(jeeringly)*: Guess you didn't aim high enough, Susan. "Not failure but low aim is crime." Remember how we had to memorize that little gem in school?

SUSAN: You seem to have remembered your homework.

HANS: You're one class member who did better than your dreams, anyway.

SUSAN: Don't be too sure. Oh, I've had an exciting life. Three husbands in place of those three kids. But even though I probably wrote it with my tongue in my cheek, that picket fence and that little cottage have something to be said for them.

FRED: Now don't you go romantic on me. You're my ideal of the successful female who shows all the men how life can be lived.

SUSAN: Yes, and where has it gotten me? I can't rest. I can't stop, or the opposition will beat me to a story. Even when life seems to give you more than you asked for, you have the feeling that someone is laughing at you.

FRED: We're not doing too well. But we have two more candidates for Mr. Success.

ABEL: You can count me out. I remember what I wrote in that silly book. I was going to be a racing car driver. Isn't that it, Mary?

MARY: That's right. And you seemed to have all the qualifications, judging by the number of traffic tickets you picked up in school.

HANS: Yes, you were Abel Harding, the Barney Oldfield of Chatham High.

ABEL *(laughing):* You should see me on my tractor, racing around a field that needs plowing. I'm no speed demon any more.

HANS: But you did drive in races for a while. I used to see your name in the paper now and then.

ABEL: Yes, I had my fling. But I never won the top races. I was just a second rater. And when my dad offered me the farm—well, here I am, the monarch of the soil rather than the racing track.

MARY: Do you miss it? The racing, I mean?

ABEL: Sometimes. I miss the noise and the excitement and the dust and the people milling around and the reporters. But a fellow can't have everything.

FRED: So much for Abel. But how about Hans?

MARY: I saved that one until last. You see, Hans wrote in the book that he wanted to be a doctor.

SUSAN: And that's what you are, Hans. A doctor.

ABEL: Hurrah. At least one in our class called the turn. One success in the crowd.

MARY: That's not too good an average. Still, it's good to know that one person picked his job and followed through on it.

HANS: Now just a minute . . . .

ABEL: Don't take away our triumph or congratulations.

HANS: Sorry, but you're acting like a crowd of idiots. I chose my job and stuck with it. You people went in other directions. So what?

FRED: You reached your goal and the rest of us failed. That's what's important.

HANS *(standing up):* No, it isn't. You're assuming that since things didn't turn out just as you planned, you're failures. But you don't know what you might have done if your dreams *had* come true. Let me tell you how things worked out for me. I did want to be a doctor, and things broke right for me. But I wanted to do big things to save humanity. Well, I ended up listening to fussy old ladies tell me all their imaginary symptoms—largely because they pay well.

MARY: I knew Hans would rob us of our last illusion.

HANS: Well, you need to have your eyes opened. What you people overlook is that the story of every human being is the story of unfinished business. Everybody makes plans, but whether things turn out right or not, the dream never comes true. We all get half-way to our goals and no farther.

ABEL: But why does it have to be like that? It seems you can't win for losing.

HANS: I've thought a lot about that, and Mary's Wish Book brings it all to mind again. I think the answer is that no one is willing to go the whole way with his life. We want our goals but we want our comforts too. We don't have the courage to go all out for what we want. So the verdict always has to be—unfinished business.

FRED *(after pause):* You know, Hans, that's a pretty

good description of life—unfinished business. That's the way mine has been, anyway. But I wonder if anybody ever did get out of life just what he planned, if anybody ever had the courage to risk all and end life like a victory.

(Blackout. Then a voice from the darkness.)

VOICE: It is finished.

The Sermon

"It is finished." John 19:30.

When a man is painting a room, there comes a time when the last dab of paint has covered the last bit of bare surface. The painter can say, "It's finished." When a man writes a book, there comes a time when he has made the last editorial change and substituted the last synonym, and he can say of his book, "It is finished." There came a time in the life of Jesus Christ when he too could say, "It is finished."

But immediately we are faced with some problems. We know what the painter is trying to do. We know what the author intends. But what had Jesus finished when he uttered this sixth word from the cross? How could he say, "It is finished," when before him were the resurrection and the ascension? Moreover, the church hadn't even been organized; the whole work of spreading the gospel remained to be done. What could he mean, "It is finished"?

Even more than that, do Jesus' words imply idleness or fruitlessness on our part? If he finished everything, is there anything for us to do? Is all our Christian activism, our busy congregational programs, our personal strivings in vain? Should we simply fold our hands and wait for our heavenly reward, since Jesus finished everything at Calvary?

The truth of the matter is that with the sixth word from the cross we are dealing with a paradox. Here is a word that finishes and that doesn't finish. Here is an ending that doesn't end. Indeed, if Jesus had never said, "It is finished," we would have less work to do. But we can see the meaning of this paradox only when we go back to our first question: What had Jesus finished?

Well, what did he come to do? The painter came to paint a room. The author sat down to write a book. *Jesus Christ came to show men how to live.* He was a demonstration, an illustration from God of what man was intended to be. Thus Jesus told us that he was the way, the truth, and the life. He declared that he had come so that men might have life, and have it more abundantly. Again and again he said that men should follow him.

Now don't misunderstand. Jesus wasn't trying to show us that we should all die on a cross or that we should wander about the countryside preaching the gospel or that none of us should get married. His example had only one point: Life is to be lived in obedience to God. The cross was only the climax, the extreme example. We know by Jesus' example that even if obedience leads to a cross, that is still the way that life is to be lived. But every step Jesus took, every word that he spoke had the same source—the will of God. That's why the Christian church has always laid such stress on what happened in the Garden of Gethsemane. There the pressure to depart from the pattern was tremendous. Yet even there Jesus was true to his purpose and could declare: "Not my will but thine be done" (Luke 22:42).

There never was any spirit of compromise in Jesus Christ. He showed men what life should be: obedience, harmony with the will of God. He "became obedient unto death: even the death of the cross," as we sing during the Lenten season. We get a little glimpse of this Christ-like nature when Abraham obeyed God and was willing to offer up his son Isaac. We can see a touch of this attitude in Joseph, who fled from the temptation offered by Potiphar's wife. But in Jesus Christ we have one who went the whole way, who obeyed to the very end. The sixth word from the cross marked the end of the example. The demonstration was complete. Men now knew how life should be lived.

Now you can see why this is an ending that doesn't end. The whole point of an example is that others should profit by it. Jesus finished his life on this earth, but you and I have ours still to live. We must live in the same way as the Master did if we are to be children of God. Of course, that's where the trouble begins. We don't find it easy to serve God in this fashion. As one of the characters in the play says, "We want our goals, but we want our comforts too." We too live lives that are full of unfinished business. We want to be religious, but not too religious. Obedience to God becomes a sometime thing. We think that God will be satisfied with half a loaf.

James McNeill Whistler, the famous artist, was once shown a drawing by an amateur. Whistler looked at it in silence; finally a friend said, "Isn't it at least tolerable?" Whistler replied: "What is your opinion of a tolerable egg?" We all know the answer to that. An egg must be fresh or it is worse than useless. A tolerable Christian isn't much good either. The Christian can't compromise as did the people in our play. Life must be lived in obedience. In the kingdom of God no compromise can imperil love or truth or goodness. Cost what it may, the Christian must also be willing to say, "Not my will but thine be done." In a poem entitled "Gethsemane" Ella Wheeler Wilcox has said it very effectively for us:

All those who journey, soon or late,
Must pass within the garden's gate;
Must kneel alone in darkness there,
And battle with some fierce despair.
God pity those who cannot say:
"Not mine but thine"; who only pray:
"Let this cup pass," and cannot see
The purpose in Gethsemane.[6]

But it is a superficial view which sees Jesus only as an illustration, an example. Important as that characteristic may be, something deeper is involved in Jesus' life. Anyone who reads the gospel record carefully is aware that a titanic conflict was being waged throughout the life of Christ, a battle between the forces of light and those of darkness. And this was no sham battle with the results assured from the start. The temptations of Jesus were real. The attacks against him were real. The lashes were real, the nails were real. The power displayed by Pilate was actual and physical, backed up by soldiers with spears and swords.

Yet Christ conquered all that his enemies could thrust at him. Unlike the characters in our play, Jesus went all-out in this battle. And when he came to the cross, this was not defeat but the proclamation to the world that there is a love stronger than death, a good that evil cannot defeat. This sixth word from Calvary is no cry of despair but a shout of triumph. Christ had beaten his enemies. They could not break his will. The struggle was finished and Satan's power was broken.

And yet not finished. The victory was won for you and me. It was not just an athletic contest between Satan and God. Jesus Christ broke the bonds of sin so that we could also be free. For as he told men in his day, "If the Son makes you free, you will be free indeed." Jesus' cry from the cross means that you will never have to be afraid again. You have been forgiven, you have been granted a new life if you have accepted Jesus Christ. Nothing in the future can defeat you. Remember how Paul gives the Romans a long list of difficulties and tribulations and then says that none of these can separate us from the love of God in Christ Jesus.

Moreover, these words can be applied to our particular and individual problems. Since Jesus has defeated the forces of evil, you and I are not prisoners of any particular sin. If you have a gossipy tongue or a bad temper, you can get rid of it. If you have doubts or times of despair, you can conquer them. The shackles have been unloosed. We are free from the tyranny of sin. I don't mean that we become perfect because of Christ's victory. But the slavery, the subjection of man's nature to evil, is gone. How well John Bunyan portrays this in *Pilgrim's Progress*. In one part of the journey, Christian and Hopeful fall under the control of Giant Grim and are in a dungeon in Doubting Castle. Suddenly Christian says, "What a fool am I thus to lie in a stinking Dungeon, when I may as well walk at liberty. I have a Key in my bosom, called Promise, that will, I am persuaded, open any Lock in Doubting Castle." [7]

That's the point of this sixth word from the cross. Jesus has won the victory and we now have the promise that we too can win the victory. These words from the cross open new vistas of life for all who accept what has been done for them. It must be noted, of course, that we must accept Christ's victory and make it ours. Only in this way can we live the victorious, the complete, life. Otherwise, we will have to echo the words of one of the characters in the play: "Even when life gives you more than you asked for, you have the feeling that someone is laughing at you." We must live in Christ or our life will be filled with unfinished business, unending regrets.

It is not hard to see why this is the ending that doesn't end. The victory of Christ is for all people and all times. As long as there remains one sinner who is still in the toils of sin, as long as men are prisoners of their own evil desires, the work of Jesus is not finished. The message must go forth, the good news must be announced so that all can profit. Just as the Salk vaccine represented the victory over polio, and yet each one must receive the shots, so Christ's victory must be shared by all.

All of us have seen pictures or representations of Christ on the cross. But there is a particular portrayal that is becoming more popular today. Christ is on the cross, but he is clothed in regal robes. He bears a real crown on his head and his face has the look of triumph upon it. There is much to be said for this representation. At least it is in harmony with the sixth word from Calvary. Our Lord is no longer crying in agony. With the sixth word, the king begins to assume his throne. Jesus has won the victory, finished his work, and opened the way to victory for all men.

The Seventh Word

"Father, into thy hands I commit my spirit."

Luke 23:46

The Trust That Isn't Misplaced

The Drama

THE CHARACTERS

LOUIS DINANT—insurance agent, not too pushy but anxious

JACK ROLAND—young business man

THE SETTING

Jack Roland's office. All that is needed are two chairs. A table or small desk can be placed in front of Jack's chair but this isn't necessary.

LOUIS *(standing up, waving insurance policy):* Jack, I promise I won't ever bother you again on this subject. But I just have to make one last effort to sell you this policy.

JACK: Now Louie, I'd like to accommodate you. Really I would. But I just can't afford it.

LOUIS: That's the point I'm trying to make with you. You can't afford not to take out this policy.

JACK: You seem to be forgetting that I've got a wife to support. Not to mention two kids.

LOUIS: That's just what I'm remembering. Look here, Jack, you and I have been friends for a long time. Now level with me. Just where would Jane be with those two kids if you should die right now?

JACK: What?

LOUIS: Just where would she be? How would she be fixed financially?

JACK: Well, I'll have to admit that she wouldn't be too well off. You know I haven't been able to save much, what with the business taking a lot of capital to get started, and everything.

LOUIS: That's the reason you need this life insurance policy. Just because you haven't been able to save much.

JACK: There's one flaw in your argument, Louie. I'm as sound as a horse. I haven't put on a pound in five years and I'm not considering cashing in my chips right now.

LOUIS *(disgustedly):* Yeah. You sound like Joe Gustaf son. *(Sits down.)*

JACK: What about Joe Gustafson?

LOUIS: A friend of yours?

JACK: I know him. He comes in here and picks up some supplies now and then. Hasn't been around for a couple of weeks, though.

LOUIS: You bet he hasn't been around. Joe Gustafson died three weeks ago.

JACK *(unbelieving):* Died? You're kidding. This is part of your sales pitch.

LOUIS: Not a bit of it. I tried to sell him a policy about a month ago and he gave me the same story you're giving me. Didn't need more insurance, was healthy as a teen-ager, and would live another fifty years. So three weeks ago he had a heart attack, and that was it. They never even got him to the hospital. That's what I'm trying to tell you, Jack. You can't afford to take a chance on yourself.

JACK *(stunned):* He really died! I guess that was when I was out of town on that business trip. That's why I didn't know about it. Joe Gustafson dead! Why he was two years younger than I am. I remember because we were talking about our birthdays one day when he was here in the office.

LOUIS: Jack, you need this policy. As a friend, let me beg you to get more insurance. I don't care whether you buy it from me or not. But you need more protection for your family.

JACK: Yes, yes, you're right.

LOUIS *(jumping up):* You mean you'll take it?

JACK: Yes, on one condition.

LOUIS *(worried):* Well, what's the condition?

JACK: That you'll sit down here and talk to me for a little while.

LOUIS *(relieved):* Oh, sure, sure. I'm not making any more calls tonight. *(Sits.)* What do you want to talk about?

JACK: Louie, I don't want you to laugh at me. But you said something a few minutes ago that really shook me up.

LOUIS: About Joe Gustafson?

JACK: No, before that. You asked me where Jane would be if I should die right now. What I want to know is—where would I be?

LOUIS: What?

JACK: That's my question. Suppose I should drop dead, right here and now. What happens then?

LOUIS: Wait a minute. You don't need me. You need a preacher.

JACK *(standing up and walking as he talks):* I don't want to talk to any preacher. Don't know any, anyway. But you talk to lots of people after someone in the family has died. What do they think's happened to the one who's dead?

LOUIS: Jack, that's a big question.

JACK: I know it. But it's been on my mind for a long time. Buried down deep but I've known it's there. What happens, what can we expect when we're dead? Tell me, if you know anything.

LOUIS: I'll do the best I can. *(Jack sits down again.)* Well, some people I talk to seem to think that when you're dead, you're dead. That's the end of it.

JACK: There's something to be said for that. No memories, no judgment, nothing. But somehow I'm not convinced that that's the right answer. Are you?

LOUIS: No. I suspect that people who believe that or who pretend to are just whistling in the dark.

JACK: Can't we do more than just whistle in that darkness?

LOUIS: Well, I went to Joe Gustafson's funeral and they sang about a Beautiful Isle of Somewhere and they talked about Joe as if he were still alive. Someone even said, "Joe knows what's going on. He's pleased with all these flowers."

JACK: Did they sound like they believed in that beautiful isle?

LOUIS: No. In fact, five minutes after the service was over they were all talking about business and things that didn't have anything to do with Joe at all. It was pretty cold, I thought.

JACK: That's the trouble. So much of what you hear about life and death and heaven is sentimental stuff. It makes people feel good for a few minutes and then that's the end of it.

LOUIS: You know, I ought to take you over to talk to my aunt.

JACK: Why? What does your aunt know?

LOUIS: I'm not really sure. She does go to church all the time. Used to try to make me go when I was a kid, but I guess she's given up on me now. But somehow she seems to have an angle on this dying business that's different.

JACK: What is she? A spiritualist or something?

LOUIS: No, no, nothing like that. Only she talks about heaven and about God taking care of her and things like that.

JACK: A religious fanatic, I suppose.

LOUIS: No, not really. She's jolly and when we have a family reunion she has a good time just like the rest of us. Only she's got something inside that the rest of the family don't seem to have.

JACK: It sounds interesting. Only, I suppose she's just putting up a good front, the way most people do. *(Up, walking around again.)* Aw, I suppose you think I'm nuts. You're the first person that I ever talked to like this in my life. And tomorrow I'll probably deny that I ever raised the subject. Only, sometimes the uncertainty seems more than a fellow can stand.

LOUIS: Why do you let it worry you?

JACK: How can I help it? A fellow works and gets his business built up, and then he dies and that's the end of it. What good did it do him? And some people never even have that much satisfaction. Some never even have a chance to grow up. Maybe they're the lucky ones. But a fellow can't help wondering what life's all about. If this is all of it, it's a pretty lousy deal.

LOUIS: Now wait a minute, Jack. You've got a good start in business and you're on the road to bigger things.

JACK: Sure I am. And if I die right now, what's it all gotten me? And if I live long enough to make my business a success, how do I know that's what my life was for? Maybe I should have been doing something else. How's a fellow to know?

LOUIS: Now you're getting me all mixed up.

JACK: That's the trouble. Any fool can ask questions. But there are never any answers.

LOUIS: Maybe you need some religion, something to believe in.

JACK: That wouldn't make it any better. How can I be sure I've got the right religion? Fellows come into the office now and then and argue about religion, but I'm no smarter when they get through than when they started.

LOUIS: Well, just pick a religion. Maybe it doesn't make any difference.

JACK: But it must make some difference. And I don't want a "maybe." I want to know what's on the other side of that curtain, death. I want something or somebody that I can put my trust in. I can trust your insurance company because they've got good assets and a good record of payments. But whom do you trust with your life?

LOUIS: You've got me. I've run out of answers.

JACK: That's the trouble. Nobody can give a fellow any help. But there must be an answer somewhere. There's got to be. I want to know what happens when a man dies. Where can he put his trust? Where? *(Sinks into chair.)*

(Blackout. Then the voice.)

VOICE: Father, into thy hands I commit my spirit.

The Sermon

"Father, into thy hands I commit my spirit." Luke 23:46.

The world always listens to the words of a dying man. Somehow we think that what a man says in the face of death is especially significant. So the final statements by criminals are given great credence. The last words of controversial figures are carefully examined. Thus when Luther came to the end of his life a friend asked him: "Reverend Father, are you willing to die in the name of the Christ and the doctrine which you have preached?" We are told that Luther's "yes" was loud enough for the whole group to hear.

It is only natural then for us to be interested in the last recorded statement of Jesus from the cross. Here should be supreme wisdom from the source of all wisdom. Unfortunately, the seventh word doesn't measure up to such expectations. Actually Jesus is again quoting from the Psalms, as he did when he spoke his fourth word. This time he is using words from Psalm 31, and the words are a familiar prayer often used by Jews in Jesus' day. This was probably equivalent in the first century to our "Now I lay me down to sleep." Jesus, we can be sure, had often said "Father, into thy hands I commit my spirit." The words are not sensational. They are ordinary.

And that's the point. Jesus, facing death, approached it in exactly the same fashion as he approached life. Death made no difference. He accepted it just as he had accepted all the events of his life—he committed everything to God. Here is an echo of the words spoken in the Garden of Gethsemane: "Not my will but thine be done." Death simply did not change Jesus' attitude, it did not disturb his faith. It just didn't make any difference, for he knew all things were safe in God's hands.

That's exactly what this seventh word should say to every Christian, to you and to me. Death doesn't make any difference. If we are children of God, then we can accept the unpleasant experience of death as we accept every other event in life. We simply commit all things into God's hands. We must have the same faith as the Apostle Paul, who insisted that it didn't make any difference whether he lived or died, since he was with the Lord either way. This is what Bishop Pike is seeking to say in his book *The Next Day:*

> Christianity offers us no escape from death, no way of hiding from it. The secret is this: The Christian Church, the Christian faith, invites you to die now. And if you die now, you'll never have to die again, in any real sense, in any ultimately disastrous sense.[8]

Now, I'm not seeking to defend an absurdity. There is a sense in which death is a fearful thing, whether a man is a Christian or not. It is an experience that no one ever relished, neither Christ nor any of his followers. Death tears a human being from his family, his friends, his possessions, his world. It plunges man into the unknown. But the Christian knows that it cannot make any real difference to him because he is safe with God. The believer can say with his Lord: "Father, into thy hands I commit my spirit."

It is the man who is alienated from God who finds death a tragedy. The figure in our play was agitated, and rightly so. Death cast a shadow over everything that seemed important in life. Death threatened to make life a shambles. The worried businessman had no assurance, no hope, no promise, no one to trust with his life. Man caught in this condition is tempted to echo the sentiment of the Welsh poet, Dylan Thomas, who wrote:

> Do not go gentle into that good night.
> Rage, rage against the dying of the light.[9]

The hopelessness, the tragedy of death moved another modern poet to begin a lyric with these words: "I am not resigned to the shutting away of loving hearts in the hard ground." [10] It is a terrible thing to die without hope.

Perhaps this is the place where the difference between Christian and non-Christian is most sharply revealed. In life, both may live in ways which are not too unalike. But to the man of the world, death is a period, the end of a sentence, the end of all. To the believer death is a comma, a pause before existence continues in greater depth. The Christian knows that all is safe in God's hands.

Thus these last words of Jesus are important, simply because they aren't important. They bring us assurance by stilling our natural fears of death. The seventh word says it is possible to face this terrible enemy without flinching. For if we are safe in God's hands now, if we can lie down and sleep safely in our bed tonight because we know God watches over us, then we can also lie down in the sleep of death without fear. For death doesn't make any difference in the life of the believer. It is simply one more episode in life.

But hang on to that word "life." For here is something that does make a difference. It is not death that is important but life. Why could Jesus die so calmly? Because the last word from the cross was an expression of his whole life. All his life he had trusted in God. He had lived with his heavenly Father, coming to him in prayer, seeking always to do his will. It was nothing new for Jesus to turn everything over to God. The relationship between Jesus and God was an old and tested relationship. So Jesus could die, sure that he would be safe with God, just as he had been all his life.

It is this truth that we must grasp. The problem is not how to die but how to live. You cannot live one way and then expect to die another way. The man in our play was making that mistake. He was worried about dying, and yet he refused to consider the subject of religion in his life. But these two things are inseparable; it's how a man lives that will determine the way he will be able to approach death. We must die with the same faith that we have possessed all during our lifetime. A certain Christian, faced with the prospect of a lingering death, said it very well. When his friends came to sympathize with him, he said, "Don't feel sorry for me. I've been preparing for this all my life."

That's the meaning behind Jesus' last word from the cross. Jesus had been preparing for his death all his life. His life had always been committed to God, so there was no difficulty in continuing that commitment at the moment of death. And the Christian can learn this secret from his Master. The answer to our natural fear of death is—life. How do you live? Whom do you trust with your life? What is God to you now?

And now we're involved in a problem. For Jesus Christ was the sinless Son of God. He was tempted as we are, but he was without sin. There had been no lapses, no wavering in his life. But you and I face a different situation. Our trust in God is often very weak. We love the things of this world too much. We slip and stumble. We are like a woman invited to a great, fashionable party who has only an old spotted dress to wear. We're afraid to say, "Father, into thy hands I commit my spirit," because too many times we have said, "Not thy will but mine be done."

And now we must take back something that was said earlier. It is true that Christ's death did not make any difference to him, for he was in God's hands whether he lived or died, but his death makes all the difference in the world for us. For Christ made atonement for our sins on that cross. He washed us clean. He was the Lamb of God, offered for all men. And when we face death we can rely on that fact. We are not going to have to stand on our own record but on Christ's. Did you ever notice how often the Scripture speaks about robes covering those who stand before God? The Book of Revelation uses that figure a number of times. The Parable of the Wedding Garment talks about a special robe for those attending the wedding. The prodigal son received a robe to cover his rags when he came home from his life of sin. All these pictures have the same meaning. You and I can have the perfect righteousness of Christ as a protection. We can stand before God, clothed in our Lord's perfection. We die as we live, surrounded by his grace.

I once saw a simple drawing that illustrated this truth very well. It showed God looking at man and man looking at God. But between the two loomed the cross of Christ. Thus God only saw man through the atonement of Christ and man only saw God in the person of his Savior on the cross. That's a true picture of the Christian life and death. We live under the forgiveness of Christ, and we die under the same protection. There is no cause for fear, only for trust in the goodness of God.

We have come all this way and now we can see where the real message of this seventh word lies. This is the story of trust, of trust that isn't misplaced. Jesus Christ trusted in God all his life, and so when the hour of death came he had no cause for anxiety. He could say, "Father, into thy hands I commit my spirit." You and I can do the same thing. We will not be perfect, but we can trust in the promises of God in Christ. By the power of the Holy Spirit we can accept the forgiveness and the new life which is offered us by our Savior. If we do, our trust will never be misplaced. We too can say when faced with death, "Father, into thy hands I commit my spirit." In the words of a beautiful Lenten hymn:

> May thy life and death supply
> Grace to live and grace to die,
> Grace to reach the home on high:
> Hear us, holy Jesus.
>
> SBH, 81

Notes

I. THE FORGIVENESS THAT DOESN'T STOP

1. Leslie D. Weatherhead: *In Quest of a Kingdom* (New York and Nashville: Abingdon-Cokesbury Press), pp. 210, 211.

II. THE POWER THAT DOESN'T FALTER

2. Hans Lilje: *The Valley of the Shadow* (Philadelphia: Fortress Press), p. 90.

III. THE CONCERN THAT NEVER CEASES

3. Thomas Hardy: *The Mayor of Casterbridge* (New York: Harper & Row, 1922), p. 345.

4. Anthony Trollope: *Can You Forgive Her?* (London: Oxford University Press), Vol. II, p. 351.

V. THE NATURE THAT DOESN'T CHANGE

5. Louis Untermeyer: *Challenge* (New York: Harcourt, Brace & World, 1914).

VI. THE END THAT DOESN'T END

6. Ella Wheeler Wilcox: "Gethsemane" (W. B. Conkey Co.).

7. John Bunyan: *Pilgrim's Progress* (Oxford: Clarendon Press), p. 145.

VII. THE TRUST THAT ISN'T MISPLACED

8. James Pike: *The Next Day* (New York: Doubleday & Co., Inc.), pp. 150, 151.

9. Dylan Thomas: *Collected Poems*. Copyright 1952 by Dylan Thomas. Reprinted by permission of New Directions Publishing Corporation.

10. From "Dirge Without Music." From *Collected Poems* (New York: Harper & Row). Copyright 1928, 1955 by Edna St. Vincent Millay and Norma Millay Ellis. By permission of Norma Millay Ellis.